4TH QUARTER FUMBLES

Keys to Finishing Strong

GLENN K. GUNDERSON JR.
with Kathy Gisi Wimbish

ΕΧulon
ELITE

4th Quarter Fumbles
Keys to Finishing Strong
by Glenn K. Gunderson Jr. with Kathy Gisi Wimbish

Photograph Courtesy of Deborah Tracey

Printed in the United States of America.

ISBN 9781498489249

Scripture quotations taken from the Holy Bible, New International Version (NIV). Copyright © 1973, 1978, 1984, 2011 by Biblica, Inc.™. Used by permission. All rights reserved.

www.xulonpress.com

DEDICATION

To Alejandro, Kiley, Clara, Emily, Jem and Avonlea ... it's because

of you that I don't want to fumble in the fourth quarter.

ENDORSEMENTS

"*Fourth Quarter Fumbles* is the definitive playbook for living in these challenging times. Gunderson mines deep truths and offers strikingly insightful lessons, principles, and disciplines to stay the course and finish strong."

Grant Thorne, Strength & Conditioning Coach,
Green Bay Packers

"It seems we all, at times, pursue the illusory idols of self-reliance, status, achievement and wealth. Perhaps this is why God warns of this in the First and Second Commandments. *In Fourth Quarter Fum*bles, Glenn Gunderson has masterfully unearthed how we can learn lessons from the lives of the kings of Israel to discover that chasing the world's idols is a dangerous game. The journeys of these kings reveal that, ultimately, we all must face the reality that our true identity and lasting legacy can be fulfilled in the grace and love of God alone. With fresh and illuminating sports metaphors, this is a book of powerful stories and insightful applications that every person of faith would profit greatly from reading. I couldn't put it down!"

Rob Pelinka, CEO of The Landmark Sports Agency
and prominent NBA Basketball Agent

"A football game is a perfect analogy for the process of life. In *Fourth Quarter Fumbles*, Glenn Gunderson utilizes poignant examples from contemporary sports and from Old Testament kings to demonstrate the challenges and opportunities we all have in living a productive, Christian life. Pastor Gunderson's creative and thought-provoking book is a must read game plan for helping us navigate and succeed in our daily Christian pursuit."

Dave Rice, UNLV Head Men's Basketball Coach 2011-2016

"All of us are destined to live our own fourth quarter. Pastor Gunderson allows us to look at some of the ancient kings of Israel and how they dropped the ball near the end of their lives. His encouragement to us: During the first three quarters of life, walk with Jesus and read his playbook. Then, stay close to Him as you play that all-important fourth quarter. Great book!"

Jim Milhon, Head Football Coach (retired),
Azusa Pacific University

"My friend Glenn Gunderson has done it again! *Fourth Quarter Fumbles* reprises the winning formula found in *Biblical Antidotes for Life's Toxins*. Reading this book will help you learn important Biblical stories, the character of the God who loves you, and the truth of how you can be victorious in life and finish well. This book not only reveals the character challenges that cause fourth quarter fumbles, it provides a clear route so that you end up winning rather than losing in life."

Dr. John Jackson, President of William Jessup University,
Author of Books on Transformational Leadership & Spiritual
Formation, and Motivational Speaker

"Glenn Gunderson is paying attention! Here is an honest, practical, and much needed book addressing an all too common occurrence among followers of Christ in America today."

Dr. William C. Nolte, Mission Lead,
Transformation Ministries

"Fourth Quarter Fumbles is a great motivator to give our best for Christ at any stage of life. Glenn uses biblical examples and his own depth of life experience to give practical guidance on how to avoid the pitfalls that can destroy our lives. This book will inspire to live for Christ right until the day You are promoted to Glory."

Dane Aaker, Lead Pastor, Centerpoint Church,
Colton, California

CONTENTS

FOURTH QUARTER FUMBLES
INTRODUCTION
TAKING THE FIELD

My name is Glenn Gunderson, and I'm a football fan.

If you met me or visited my church, you'd quickly learn that my passion for sports runs deep. In fact, I can't recall a time when sports were not a big part of my life. I never played football (way too scrawny!) but ran the 1500 meters in high school, college, and on an American team in Eastern Europe.

It's important for me to tell you about my lifelong interest in sports. Not so much because it gives you insight into who I am, but more, because of how God has used this enjoyable outlet to teach me profound spiritual lessons. Lessons that have helped me grow in my faith and build spiritual muscle. Lessons I believe God would like me to share with you for the same purpose in your life. That's why I'm writing this book.

As I was preparing for a series of sermons on the kings of Israel, I kept thinking of these men as players on a football field. To be honest, quite a few of them were such poor leaders and so lacking in their commitment to the Lord that they got cut from God's team. The legacy they leave behind is a sad one of failure, both personally and spiritually. However, in others, I saw a pattern. These kings started out well. They were men who knew God and sought to build their kingdoms on His principles. They were stars on His playing field—for most of their lives. Yet, sadly, they made poor choices late in the game. You might say, they "fumbled" in the fourth quarter of their lives.

CLUMSY KINGS

In this book, you'll meet a dozen "clumsy kings." Their stories can be found in God's history book, the Bible—primarily in 1 and 2 Chronicles and 1 and 2 Kings. At the beginning of each chapter, I've referenced the biblical chapters that tell about the king you'll be studying. Before you begin reading my chapter, you will find it helpful to read the biblical references in your favorite translation or paraphrase. (By the way, unless I mention otherwise, I'll be using the New International Version as I highlight scripture in the coming chapters.)

Now, even though I can't imagine it, I do realize that there are many people in this world who don't share my passion for sports! If you are one of those people, please keep reading anyway. Perhaps football isn't your thing. Your passion may be music, art, cooking, reading, gardening, parenting—anything. No matter what you enjoy, I think you will agree that it's important to do your best and finish well.

I believe that God recorded the stories of these kings in the Bible because He wants to use them to teach us something. As we examine their strengths and then look together at their fourth quarter fumbles, we can see what happened that caused them to drop the ball. As God coaches us through this study, we'll identify their weaknesses and see how they could have avoided the pitfalls in their lives. In this way, perhaps, we can avoid similar pitfalls in our own lives.

STRATEGIC CHOICES

Every one of the kings we will look at in this book loved God and made a deliberate choice to follow Him. As long as they followed

His "coaching," they remained spiritually strong. God blessed them with victorious lives and used them as mighty leaders. Sadly, though, somewhere along the line, these monarchs also made a choice to take their eyes off of God. They got out of shape spiritually and the "muscles" of their faith turned to flab. They neglected to apply the principles and strategies God had given to help them play on His team without compromise. They fumbled and fell, leaving generations behind them to groan from the sidelines. It didn't have to be that way. With God's help, they could have finished victoriously and left a winning legacy, and that brings me to the main point of this book:

> *God has given us a play-by-play record in the Bible of Israel's kings to help us avoid their disappointing fourth quarter fumbles. Rather than scoring a "touchdown," they were "taken down" by their own poor choices. If we learn from their mistakes, we can live victorious lives—from start to finish!*

TIME OUT

Now let's take time out for a brief look at how these men came to be kings in the first place. Thousands of years before Jesus was born, God chose Abraham to be the father of the Israelites. Through the lineage of this man's family, *HIS*tory would unfold.

It was not God's original plan for Abraham's heirs to be governed by human kings. He would have preferred to remain their benevolent and perfect Father-ruler. But God would not compromise His righteous standard of living, and men would not live by it. With every passing generation, human nature became more and more "self" focused.

In Judges 21:25 (KJV) it says that the time came when "every man did that which was right in his own eyes." Think about that for just a moment. In your own family, what would life be like if everyone did what he saw fit? Would it be peace and harmony all the time? I doubt it, because, when sin came into the world, it brought selfishness along with it. Ever since, it's been "all about me."

To make a long story short, the Israelites decided that their own ways were better than God's. Eventually, they rejected God as their coach and demanded a human king. This is where it gets a little bit tricky for me! You see, I want you to know enough about the big picture of this historical time to see that it was a time of steady drifting away from God. Instead of order and justice, there was violence and chaos. The overwhelming majority of the kings were not only complacent and disinterested in God, they were downright evil. The consequences of their ungodly leadership were devastating. Under these kings, Israel became so wicked in God's sight that He decided there should no longer be a Kingdom of Israel. He allowed the kingdom of Babylon to overtake and destroy them, taking captive a remnant of survivors.

THE FAMILY TREE

Perhaps you've read the book by C.S. Lewis entitled *The Lion, the Witch and the Wardrobe*. This is the first of six allegorical adventures that comprise Lewis' classic series *The Chronicles of Narnia*. It is an exciting story about an evil queen, three children who rise up to fight her, and a good lion who rescues them from her deadly grasp. The chronicles of the Bible make for the same sort of exciting reading. But while adventures in Narnia are allegorical fantasy, those in the Bible are historical reality.

It's important to know that there was an uprising during the reign of Israel's fourth king, Rehoboam. This uprising resulted in splitting the kingdom. The northern kingdom of Israel consisted of ten tribes. Two tribes in the south became the kingdom of Judah. The books of Chronicles are all about the early kings in Judah—the kings who came from the line of David.

Throughout this book, we'll be looking closely at the stories recorded in Chronicles. As we do, I want you to think of it as being like the family tree of Jesus. Looking at the snapshots of the personalities in these stories is like looking into His own ancestral album. Just like any family tree, some bad apples fell from this one. There are stories of men, women, and even some young children who brought their own leadership style to the family. There's even a wicked queen that makes Narnia's white witch seem tame, but there are also some encouraging stories.

THE GOOD, THE BAD, AND THE UGLY

Like I said, I want you to have a glimpse of the big picture to help you understand and analyze the "snapshots" of the kings we will be looking at in the coming chapters. However, I don't want you to get bogged down by the historic details. The monarchy begins in 1000 BC with King David. It ends in 586 BC with Zedekiah. Take a count and you'll find that there were twelve bad kings and ten good kings. But most of the good kings had experiences that I'm calling "fourth quarter fumbles." You'll learn about them in detail— the good, the bad, and the ugly—as you read through the chapters of this book. We'll look at it all, because we can learn from every type of experience.

GETTING IN THE GAME

Are you with me so far? I hope so, because we're almost ready to kick off our study. Before we do, here's something for you to ponder. The lessons in this book are based on the premise that *you* are on God's team. Have you stepped onto the field of faith by a deliberate choice to receive Jesus into your heart? If you have, God is your coach. You have His playbook, the Bible, to teach and guide you.

When the game gets rough, you have the Holy Spirit to encourage and uphold you. You have a team of fellow believers to encourage and help you put forth your personal best all the days of your life. And, even when you fumble, you have Jesus to redeem your mistakes.

If you are on God's team, this book is definitely for you. If not, it may not make much practical sense until you get in the game. I urge you to do that now. (This is one time when it may be wise to read the end at the beginning!) Take a few minutes to turn to the last chapter, read it with an open mind and spirit and ask God to help you receive Jesus into your heart. Then, come back to the beginning, and you'll be ready to go.

Whether you are new to God's team or a veteran, all of God's players need a workout plan. That's why I've included an application section called Playing by the Book at the end of each chapter with practical suggestions and hands-on exercises to help you stay in good spiritual shape.

SIDELINE SIDEBARS

Here's one more sidebar before we begin. There are a few things I'd like you to keep in mind as you read this book chapter by chapter. First, this is not intended to be an historical study. While we will be looking at Judah's kings within the context of the times when they reigned, our goal is to learn from their individual lives. Think of each chapter as a separate character study. This is important to remember, especially if you will (as I hope) be simultaneously reading the stories of these men as they are recorded in the Bible. If you don't bear this in mind, you may be confused at times, because we will be looking at these kings in loose chronological order.

This is good news if you are like me and don't have hours at a time to read, or you are the leader of a Bible study or small group, and would like to use this as a group study guide. You see, each chapter can stand alone. You can read and study as you have time, and you can stop to ponder the lessons learned in each chapter for as long as you like.

Having said that, here's a second sidebar. While each chapter stands alone, there is a big picture that will evolve. Again, we can draw upon the analogy of a football game that is broken up into four quarters but comes together in the end. Hang in there with me—stay in the game! I think you'll finish feeling satisfied that the lessons you've gleaned will be relevant for the rest of your life.

END ZONE CELEBRATION

It's the fourth quarter. With seconds to play, the quarterback calls time out. Heads together, leaning forward in a circle, the team is in a huddle. A word, a signal, and they know what to do. Each player has his role. They're working together like a well-oiled machine. He has the ball now and he's running towards the goal. Nothing can stop him. The crowd is on their feet. When he crosses over that line, the cheers are like thunder. Glancing to the sidelines, he sees his coach— smiling, approving, hands raised. That's when he breaks into the end zone celebration.

Football is only a game, but there are a lot of similarities to life. When I cross that line at the end of my game, I want to see a smile on my coach's face. I want to dance into His presence and hear Him say, "Well done, Glenn! You're a good and faithful servant."

I'm sure you want that too, but let's be very clear about one thing. In the game of life, it's not about "winning and losing." Jesus has already won the trophy for you. You're going to cross that goal someday. What will make the difference between a quiet welcome and a victory celebration? It's about how you play—God's way, not your own way. That reminds me of a great football story.

It was Sunday, February 4, 2007. Super Bowl Sunday. This one goes down in sports history as the day the Indianapolis Colts won the big game—and their coach, Tony Dungy, became the first black head coach to ever win a Super Bowl. The rainy weather posed uncomfortable challenges to the players, prompting one reporter to call it "Souper Bowl." But to fans who admire Tony's faith, it seemed like God was raining down blessings from Heaven.

When the clock ran out, the scoreboard flashed the numbers. 29-17, Colts. In the stands, the crowd went wild! In living rooms, restaurants, hospital beds, sports bars, airport terminals, and cars and trucks, millions of viewers and listeners joined in. For players and fans, it was a sweet, sweet victory. For Tony Dungy, it was more. This is a man who has endured tough times—both in his professional and personal lives—including the death of both parents and his son's tragic suicide. Through it all, Tony kept on coaching—for the love of the game. Even more, for the love of the Lord.

You see, Tony Dungy "plays" on another great team under the direction of the true super coach. His name is Jesus Christ, and Tony looks to Him for every strategy—in the game of football and the game of life. He finishes well because he plays God's way, without compromising.

God is a coach without compromise. Are you playing by His rules?

FOURTH QUARTER FUMBLES

CHAPTER 1

SAUL, DAVID, AND SOLOMON

THE STARTING LINEUP

They called it The Fumble

November 19, 1978: Philadelphia Eagles vs. New York Giants. With thirty-one seconds to play, the Giants were leading 17-12 and had the ball on the 29-yard line. Their quarterback, Joe Pisarcik, had it made in the shade; or, so he thought.

To clinch the win, all Joe needed to do was take a knee. Instead, he decided to hand off the ball to teammate Larry Csonka—a handoff that was fumbled.

A collective groan echoed through the stadium, as stunned Giants coaches, players and fans watched Eagles lineman Herman Edwards grab the ball and race into the endzone. It was a turnaround victory for the Eagles. ("New York Giants: Miracle in the Meadowlands")

In football, you win some and lose some. One loss shouldn't be a big deal, but, unfortunately, Joe Pisarcik was remembered for the rest of his career for this one game that Giants fans simply call The Fumble. ("New York Giants: Miracle in the Meadowlands")

For me, part of the excitement of football is anticipating a good game. I always have my favorite players—the rising stars, the proven veterans. Their talent and potential are awesome, and it's magical to watch them take the field and play their hearts out. As the big game approaches, my hopes soar. I can't wait to see who is in the starting lineup!

In this chapter, we will look at the lives of the "starter" kings of Israel: Saul, David, and Solomon. These first three kings are the most famous, and also the ones whose stories are most elaborately told in the Bible—covering many pages of the books of Samuel, Kings and Chronicles in the Old Testament. Even though it will take a little extra time, I encourage you to do a thorough reading of these Bible stories. (See *Read All About It* at the beginning of this chapter.) That way, you'll have an understanding of the big picture of the lives of Saul, David and Solomon, and the key roles they played in history. Frankly, an entire book could be written about each of these men. There is so much to learn from their experiences, but for the purposes of finding the keys to finishing our own lives well, I will be focusing on selected highlights.

Before we begin, let me give you a few facts to help place these stories in historical context. As I've already mentioned, God's original plan for His people was a theocracy with God Himself ruling as Lord and King. When the Israelites persisted in demanding a human king, God finally granted their wish; He even recruited the starters. Of course, since God is omniscient, He knew in detail about the strengths and weaknesses of these first three kings. He knew they would not be perfect leaders, and that their "fumbles" would have a long-reaching impact on future generations. He also knew that, if any men could succeed, they could. These were the best available men for the starting lineup of Israel's monarchy.

Another point to keep in mind is that during the years from 1095-975 BC when Saul, David, and Solomon were on the throne, Israel was a united kingdom. Then the kingdom broke into the northern section, which retained the name of Israel, and the southern kingdom, called Judah. Each of the starter kings ruled for 40 years.

I think we're ready now. Let the games begin!

SAUL:

THE KICKOFF KING

If kings wore jerseys, Saul's would bear the number "1." He was the very first king of Israel—the man God reluctantly recruited to kick off the next 509 years. God had warned Israel that having a king would bring more burdens than blessings, but they were stubbornly insistent. So He finally let them have what they asked for, and chose Saul to be the first king.

The Bible says that Saul was "an impressive young man without equal among the Israelites" (1 Samuel 9:2). He was exceptionally tall, strong, and a skilled soldier. This was crucial because Israel was constantly threatened by pagan nations who were bigger and had vast armies of troops. To keep Israel on the map, they needed a good military man.

As I said before, an entire book could be devoted to a study of the life and times of Saul. What I want to emphasize is how, in the beginning, this man had everything going for him—so much talent, impressive credentials, and a firm foundation of faith. Israel's first king made a good start, and here are a few of the reasons why:

Saul was humble. When God sent Samuel, the priest, to anoint Saul as king, Saul thought there must be a mistake. His response, recorded in 1 Samuel 9:21, suggests that he felt totally unworthy. "But am I not a Benjamite, from the smallest tribe of Israel, and is not my clan the least of all the clans of Benjamin?" he said. When God is looking for leaders, I believe humility is one of the qualities he wants to see on their resume. That's because a humble leader will be more likely to rely on Him and not be so quickly inclined to do things "my way."

Saul was filled with God's spirit. 1 Samuel 10:9 tells us that "God changed Saul's heart." Once Saul was convinced that God was calling him, he submitted and was anointed by the priest Samuel. The Bible says that "the Spirit of God came upon him [Saul] in power" (1 Samuel 10:10). This change in Saul was so noticeable to others that people questioned it with skepticism. When God changed your heart, were you teased? Maybe your co-workers called you a Jesus freak, or placed bets on how long it would take for you to fall back into your old ways. This kind of reaction from the world is common when God transforms a life. We should see it as a good thing because it means people can see God's spirit at work in us—changing and molding us into people who credibly reflect His character and attributes.

Saul mobilized the people against injustice. Early in Saul's reign, his passion for justice was revealed when the city of Jabesh-Gilead came under siege. The Ammonites surrounded the city and issued a startling decree. To secure a truce, every person in the city would be required to have their right eye gouged out. Of course, the people of Jabesh-Gilead sent out an urgent cry for help. When Saul heard about this barbaric outrage, the Bible says that God's spirit came upon him and "he burned with anger" (1 Samuel 11:6). He called out the troops—330,000 men from all throughout Israel—and led them out to deliver Jabesh-Gilead from the brutal enemy.

In this story, Saul's response is a good example of righteous anger. As Christians, we often feel guilty when anger gets the best of us. However, it's important to understand that anger, in itself, is not a sin. It's a natural emotion. How we process it determines whether it's right or wrong. The Bible says that Saul's anger was imparted to him by God's own spirit, so it could not be wrong or inappropriate. Today, as was true then, there are times when it is perfectly appropriate to be angry. When the Holy Spirit prompts us to respond to an injustice, we should follow Saul's example and take action. God wants us to mobilize our emotions to change the world for Christ.

Here's something to think about: There are more than 1,000 references to injustice in the Bible. That's a red flag! When God mentions something once, He wants us to pay attention. How much more He must want us to listen if He says something a thousand times. When God repeats Himself, it's because He's talking about something close to His heart. Something He wants us to take to heart—like defending the victims of injustice. Acting in concern for others is an important part of being a follower of Jesus.

Saul gave God the credit. After this incident, Saul was suddenly a hero. Some of his toughest critics became his most outspoken advocates. Now that he had proven himself, they pushed him to use his power to take revenge on the victimizers. In those days and times, this would be a logical next step. Instead, Saul took the spotlight off himself and pointed out that God was really the one who rescued them, and only God had the right to revenge. "No one shall be put to death today, for this day the Lord has rescued Israel," he said (1 Samuel 11:13). And so, instead of a vicious bloodbath, a celebration was held. It was a great victory and a great day.

If Saul had continued to exhibit attributes like these, his reign would have been glorious from start to finish. Unfortunately, he had a few human flaws. As Saul began to rely more on himself and less on God, he fumbled. One fumble led to another, like a domino effect.

There were three weak areas that tarnished Saul's record and ulti-mately took him down:

Saul repeatedly disobeyed God and did not wait for His timing.
If I had to identify Saul's greatest weakness, this would be it. Like so many people, Saul had a desire to do the right thing. But living a godly life is not just about doing the right thing. It's about doing the right thing, in the right way, at the right time. Saul had a ten-dency to run ahead of God when he felt squeezed by circumstances. Let me cite just one example, recorded in 1 Samuel 13:7-14. Saul's troops were ready and waiting to fight the Philistines, but God spoke through Samuel, the priest. He clearly instructed Saul to wait until Samuel could come and offer a sacrifice for God's blessing on the military operation. As they waited for Samuel's arrival, the troops got restless. Some began to scatter, and Saul felt anxious and pres-sured. As circumstances spun out of control, so did Saul, and he made a very bad judgment call. You see, Saul wanted God's blessing but he didn't want to wait for it. So he stepped over the line and offered the sacrifice himself. Please understand that in those days, only a priest was allowed to make a sacrifice like this. Saul was ignoring a sacred boundary. Because this decision was willful, arrogant, and demonstrated a lack of trust in God, the consequences were severe. When Samuel finally arrived upon this sad scene, he delivered this stern message: "You have not kept the command the Lord your God gave you; If you had, he would have established your kingdom over Israel for all time. But now your kingdom will not endure" (1 Samuel 13:13-14a).

There is such an important lesson for all of us in this story—a lesson to trust God and wait for His timing. Sometimes that's hard, isn't it? When there is something we want so badly—a house, a career, the desire to marry or have a child—it's very common, even for Christians, to rush ahead of God. However, without exception, it's always better to wait for God's timing. Even though God might very well want you to have that thing you desire so deeply, He may have His reasons for making you wait for it. Perhaps He knows you will savor and treasure it all the more when He gives it to you. Saul didn't wait. He jumped ahead of God, and then he compounded his sin by blaming Samuel, saying that the priest's delay forced his hand. As you'll soon see, God took Saul out of the lineup and sent in a man named David—a man whose best strength was patient trust. Keep this story in mind next time you feel impatient because you want something and God seems to be turning you a deaf ear. Wait on Him. You'll see! In the long run, waiting will be worth it.

Saul became obsessed with jealousy. Another fatal flaw was Saul's increasingly obsessive jealousy of David, the man God chose to be his successor. If you read the whole story of Saul and David, you'll see it's a sad one. Their relationship began strong. Young David was one of Saul's biggest fans. All he wanted was to serve under Saul and contribute what he could to making him a successful king. Saul could have taken David under his wing, mentored him, and ultimately been credited as the one who trained King David, the ancestor of Jesus, the king of all kings. But as David's accomplishments began to be publicly recognized, the accolades he received angered Saul. 1 Samuel 18:7 records how the women sang, "Saul has slain his thousands, and David his tens of thousands." In the tradition of Hebrew poetry, these women were actually applauding Saul and David as a team. But Saul chose to take this the wrong way. The green-eyed monster of jealousy began to consume Saul, and David was forced to run for his life.

If you have ever experienced obsessive jealousy or observed it in the lives of others, you know it can tear people apart. In my own life, I am grateful to have had an example in my own father of someone who could have behaved after the fashion of Saul, but chose not to. My dad was the co-founder and co-president of a lumber company in Virginia. When he reached his 50s, he had built a prosperous and successful business and began to think about transition to the next generation. In a very deliberate way, my father spent the next ten years searching Virginia for the top young guys in the lumber business.

He found several men who were young, aggressive, and hungry and brought them on board. Then he spent his early 60s mentoring and training these men. By the time my dad was 65, these recruits were ready to take over. My father walked away to spend his last years hunting, fishing, and collecting stock dividends. If anyone dared to say a critical word about his successors, Dad was their biggest champion. This is the role model I want to follow as I grow older, not the one we see in Saul.

Saul became involved in the occult. Towards the end of his life, as Saul felt the kingdom slipping through his fingers, he sought advice from a medium. He knew better, as the most ancient scriptures warn about how offensive this is to God. I can't overstress how dangerous it is to dabble in the occult. Today this is something that pulls so many people into the dark side. You may not think this would happen to you, but be careful. The lure of the occult can be very subtle. I recently read a startling statistic that three out of four teenagers admit they've experimented with witchcraft or psychic activities. The Bible says we must avoid any connection with these evil practices because they are like an open invitation to Satan, giving him permission to mess with our minds. Deuteronomy 18:12-13 says that "Anyone who does these things is detestable to the Lord" and that we "must be blameless" to Him. The only way to be blameless to God is to obey Him.

Over the course of time, these areas of weakness chipped away at Saul. Although he reigned for a good many years after his fumble, God was not with him. Saul became increasingly depressed and paranoid. It's not surprising that his day of reckoning came on a battlefield. It was a fatal day, not just for Saul, but for three sons who died fighting alongside him. Badly wounded by an enemy arrow, Saul knew he could not survive and asked his weapon bearer to put him out of his misery. But the soldier would not, and Saul ended up taking his own life.

NEXT UP: DAVID

Soon after Saul's suicide, God's king-elect got the news. David had been running from Saul for years, and you might think he would have rejoiced to hear that his jealous rival was dead. But David sincerely loved Saul and knew he had been called and anointed by God. His heart was broken over the way things had turned out. He led his troops in respectful mourning, then took his place as king.

It might be safe to say that no other king in history had a stronger start than David. The Bible calls him "a man after God's own heart." Let me tell you a few reasons why.

David was a man of faith. From the time he was a little boy until the time he died, David loved God passionately. Faith took root early—during those years when David was a boy shepherd, alone and tending his father's flocks. These were the formative years when God built David's faith like a muscle to prepare him for the later challenges of his life. When wild animals threatened the sheep in David's flock, he risked his life to protect them, and trusted God to protect him. In small and big ways, David looked to the Lord as his source of help, guidance, protection, and provision. God never let him down. As the boy David grew to be a man, he became strong in body, mind, and spirit.

David trusted God and not his natural abilities. Have you ever known anyone who seemed to have more than their fair share of natural talent? Think of that person multiplied ten times and you'll have an idea what kind of guy David was. The word "outstanding" doesn't come close to describing him. Here was a man who was a poet, a musician, good-looking, charismatic, a mighty soldier and leader, and a capable administrator and organizer. David might well have been the most gifted person in world history, other than Jesus. Yet, David was also extremely humble. He never took his gifts for granted, nor even thought to take credit for them. David knew his strength was a gift from God and always made sure he relied on Him and not on his own natural abilities. Whenever I read about David, I am reminded of one of my favorite verses from the Bible. It's Proverbs 21:31, and it goes like this: *"The horse is made ready for the day of battle, but victory rests with the Lord."*

It's important to use our talents and abilities to prepare for the things we face in life, but it's even more important to trust God and acknowledge that He holds every day of our lives in His capable hands. This was the key to David's close relationship with God—and it's the key to living the Christian life today.

David's main goal in life was God's glory. Perhaps the most well-known story connected with David is the account of his confrontation with a giant named Goliath. Even unbelievers love to hear how a young boy, small and armed with only a slingshot, took down an oversized bully. I value this story because it's such a great example of how God's "power is made perfect in weakness" (1 Corinthians 10:13). All David cared about when he faced the giant was that "the whole world will know that there is a God in Israel" (1 Samuel 17:46). Throughout his entire life, this desire to bring glory to God was David's primary goal. It should be ours, too.

David was humble. Although David had many human failings, he had many more spiritual successes. Why did this man have such stellar moments? I've thought prayerfully about this, and I believe it was because David was a worshiper at heart. When he got alone with God, worship was not just a warm-up. Worship was David's spiritual workout. He put heart and soul into knowing and loving God, and this kept him humble and trusting.

David was connected with others who were "sold out" to God. Throughout David's life, he cultivated relationships with people who shared his devotion to the Lord. The most notable of these friends was Jonathan, one of Saul's sons. This man who was "closer than a brother" (Proverbs 18:24) was also someone who held David accountable for his faith. It could even be debated that Jonathan's death left David floundering and vulnerable to temptation when it came in the form of a beautiful woman named Bathsheba. There is an important warning here for us. To remain strong, we need to be connected to others who will remind us of our commitment to live by God's standards. When we become isolated from the body of Christ, it's like a football player going out to play without helmet or padding. He may be a great athlete, but he's going to stagger and fall when he runs into 240 pounds of muscle in motion.

David was willing to wait for God's timing. Unlike Saul, who constantly ran ahead of God, David is known for his patient waiting on God. An example of this is a story found in 1 Samuel 24 of how Saul, intent on killing David, took 3,000 men out on a manhunt. While on this death search, Saul went into a cave to use the bathroom—never suspecting that David and his men were inside. What a temptation this was for David, who was surely tired of being on the run. He could have ended it right then and there, but he chose not to—although he did play a little mind game with Saul by sneaking up on him and cutting off a piece of his robe. As the story is told, "Afterward David was conscience-stricken . . . He said to his men, 'The Lord forbid that I should do such a thing to my master, the Lord's anointed.'" And so the years of waiting went on for David. In fact, he waited 22 long years from his anointing at 16 until his coronation after Saul's death. (Now there's a good story to remember next time you're crawling along in bumper-to-bumper traffic on the freeway!)

I've mentioned only six of David's many fine attributes. These qualities alone explain why 1 Samuel 18:14 says, "In everything he [David] did he had great success, because the Lord was with him." Even so, when David hit mid-life, he went through a perilous period when he drifted far from God's purpose for him. I'm sure you are familiar with the story of David's fatal attraction to beautiful Bathsheba. It began with an admiring look and ended in a murderous cover-up.

But the affair was merely a sad symptom of a much deeper underlying unrest. From 2 Samuel 11:1 we learn that, "In the spring, at the time when kings go off to war . . . David remained in Jerusalem." In other words, the king took time off. When he did, David lost his eternal focus. He took his eyes off of his life goal, the driving purpose that had defined his life since boyhood—to live for God and bring honor to His name. At a time when David probably thought he was strongest, he gave in to weakness. He dropped the ball.

There was another problem area that surfaced during this mid-life season. In 2 Samuel 13-18, we get an inside glimpse at David's household—and it's not a pretty sight. You see, despite his fine leadership qualities, David was not very good at parenting. He simply didn't have the same commitment to fatherhood that he did to kingship. Perhaps David thought if he was really faithful to God in his role as king, then God would take care of the home front. If you are a parent, you know it doesn't work that way. Once you become a father or a mother, raising that child for the Lord is the most important commitment you have in life—for the rest of your life. It takes time, effort and lots of diligent prayer. David's son Absalom grew up wild and rebellious, and he eventually broke David's heart.

Another mighty man of God who experienced heartbreak over his son was someone I deeply admire—the beloved evangelist, Billy Graham. I read once that when Billy and his wife Ruth were starting out in ministry as a young married couple, Ruth said, "You go out and preach the gospel and I'll raise a family you'll be proud of." But you know, even the best mother can't take the place of a father. God designed the family to have both mom and dad in unique roles of leadership. The Grahams, like David, learned this the hard way, but fortunately their son eventually followed Billy into ministry. David was not so fortunate with his son, who died young in a tragic way.

The lesson we need to learn from David's mid-life crisis is a bitter pill to swallow. Living the Christian life in a secular world does not allow us the freedom to take time off. Nor are we exempt from the consequences of not living up to what God requires of us as parents. If King David could trip and fall over these stumbling blocks, so can we.

I'm glad to say that there's a happy ending to this story. After his mid-life fumble, David recovered his spiritual stride and made a remarkable comeback. And once again we see a striking contrast between David and Saul. Unlike the first king, David did not try to blame anyone for his mistakes. When God sent a messenger named Nathan to confront David, he listened and took responsibility for his actions. His apology to God in Psalm 51 is a model of heartfelt contrition. I imagine that David was choking back tears when he cried out to God, "Against you, you only, have I sinned and done what is evil in your sight" (Psalm 51:4). God heard the sincerity in David's confession, just as He does when we cry out in regret over our sins. Like a father who has reprimanded a misbehaving child, He forgave David, and they moved on, together.

As for his weak parenting, we know that David learned from his mistakes and applied more skillful methods in raising his youngest son Solomon. Even from his deathbed, David seized every opportunity to be a "father mentor" and point his son (and Israel's third king) towards God. And, because David took responsibility for his areas of weakness, God helped him to finish his life well. Even more wonderful is the fact that He gave David's family the highest honor of being the ancestors of Jesus. His legacy on earth made a heavenly impact that continues to draw people into the family of God through faith in King Jesus, David's descendent.

SOLOMON: THE WISE KING

When David's days on earth were over, his son Solomon became the third king of Israel. Wisdom and wealth were to be the hallmarks of Solomon's rule. Like the first two kings, Solomon came on strong. As I mentioned, David invested his last years in training his son to lead as he had—with the goal of glorifying God. Here's how *The Message* paraphrases David's last wishes:

> When David's time to die approached, he charged his son Solomon, saying, "I'm about to go the way of all the earth, but you—be strong; show what you're made of! Do what God tells you. Walk in the paths he shows you." (1 Kings 2:1-2, The Message)

Solomon took this charge to heart. 2 Chronicles 1:7 tells how God came to Solomon and said, "Ask for whatever you want me to give you." Imagine! A carte-blanche invitation from God. What would you ask for? What Solomon asked for was wisdom and knowledge to be a good leader over the kingdom of Israel. His request was not only smart, it was selfless—and this pleased God immensely. You see, in God's eyes, a good leader is a servant-leader. One who sees his role as an opportunity to bless others. A bad leader, on the other hand, may misuse his authority in order to bless himself. One is "blessed to be a blessing," while the other is "blessed to be blessed."

God was very pleased with Solomon's smart request! So pleased that He not only made Solomon wise, but also wealthy. This story is an example of what is called the First Fruits principle. Basically this principle suggests that when God is first in our lives, everything else falls into place. It's not about "name it and claim it." It's about loving God and receiving all He wants to give you as you trust Him with every aspect of your life. Solomon launched his reign on this principle, and God responded by blessing him with wealth, riches, honor and reputation—more than any other king in history.

Solomon built God's temple. One of the most notable achievements of Solomon's reign was the building of the temple in Jerusalem. This had been a dream of his father David, but God had made it clear that His house was not to be built by a warrior king who had shed blood. However, God did give David the pleasure and privilege of drawing up the elaborate blueprints. David later passed them to Solomon with instructions to carry them out to the last detail. When the sacred project was finished, God appeared to Solomon and said, "I . . . have chosen this place for myself as a temple for sacrifices" (2 Chronicles 7:12).

Solomon was mission-minded. Once the temple was complete, Solomon told God that he wanted to invite the world to see it. This was not about flaunting his opulent wealth or showing off his architectural achievement. As Solomon said to God, his desire to invite foreigners to see the temple was "so that all the peoples of the earth may know your name and fear you, as do your own people Israel" (2 Chronicles 6:32-33).

Solomon's wise leadership blessed his own people and the entire known world. As Israel prospered under Solomon's lead, the world heard about it. Dignitaries like the Queen of Sheba traveled great distances to meet the wise king and to see the glorious temple. When the Queen of Sheba met Solomon and saw with her own eyes what she had heard about, she confirmed that Solomon had accomplished what he hoped for. Impressed, the Queen said, "Praise be to the Lord your God, who has delighted in you and placed you on his throne as king to rule for the Lord your God" (2 Chronicles 9:8).

As you can see, Solomon's reign was a time of promise and prosperity in Israel that can be summed up in this passage:

> King Solomon was greater in riches and wisdom than all the other kings of the earth. The whole world sought audience with Solomon to hear the wisdom God had put in his heart. (1 Kings 10:23-24)

You might be thinking right now that this sounds too good to be true, and, sadly, you would be right. When someone has climbed to the heights Solomon reached, it's a long way down if you topple, and he did. Solomon made four key mistakes that caused his downfall.

Solomon ignored God's clear cut warning. As we've seen, Solomon and God were on speaking terms. God walked and talked with him, giving clear instructions that could have prevented Solomon from wandering off track. The more you study God's Word, the more you will notice that God's promises are often accompanied by a warning. Here's what He warned Solomon:

> "As for you, if you walk before me as David your father did, and do all I command, and observe my decrees and laws, I will establish your royal throne, as I covenanted with David your father . . . But if you turn away and forsake the decrees and commands I have given you and go off to serve other gods and worship them, then I will uproot Israel from my land." (2 Chronicles 7:17-20)

This is a good warning for all of us to keep in mind in our Christian walk. Unfortunately, Solomon did not heed this—in several key areas of his life.

Solomon did not protect himself from negative influences in his inner circle. In our church, we talk a lot about oikos, a Greek word that refers to a group of about 8 to 10 people in a person's circle of influence. These are immediate and extended family members and personal friends—people God has placed close together. It's important that this inner circle include some people who are ***not*** Christians because, if we only mix with Christians, it narrows or even eliminates our influence as believers. It's like all the salt is in the salt shaker and none is out seasoning the world with Christ.

Within the oikos is a core group of 2 or 3 people who influence us. This is the inner circle I am referring to with regard to Solomon. It's absolutely crucial that these people who are closer to us than anyone else—especially spouses—share our love and passionate commitment for Christ. These few are the loved ones who have the power to steer us like beacons. If they are not aligned with us in faith, they can steer us off course.

This is what happened to Solomon—and I hope you are sitting down because what I am about to tell you will knock your socks off. Solomon had 700 wives of royal birth. (Yes, 700!) And that's not all. He also had 300 concubines. That computes to 1,000 women in his harem. (How could this happen to such a wise man?) But let's just forget about the numbers. Even if Solomon had been monogamous, the real problem was something else. The real problem was that these wives and lovers were worshipers of idols and the occult.

What was Solomon thinking? Perhaps, like so many of us, he was thinking that his faith was strong enough to be unshakable. However, time has a way of tearing down our defenses. Scripture records that "as Solomon grew old, his wives turned his heart after other gods" (1 Kings 11:4).

Solomon's excesses undermined his commitment to God. Raised by David, personally befriended by God—Solomon knew what scripture said. He was familiar with chapters like Deuteronomy 17 which specifically prohibits acquiring great numbers of horses, taking many wives, or accumulating large amounts of silver and gold. In essence, God commanded his people to be temperate because He knew the distractions that would come with the accumulation of things. God wanted to be all-sufficient to His people, and even the king was to be subservient. Solomon ignored this well-known passage and indulged himself. You might summarize his downfall in three words: self, sex, and silver. In and of themselves, these are not bad. But when these things (or anything) become more important in our lives than God, we are sure to stumble.

Solomon did not repent when God "turned up the heat." As Solomon staggered through his bad fourth quarter, God did not just stand back and watch him go down. He raised up adversaries to get Solomon's attention. Sometimes God has to do this in order to shake us loose and remind us of our need for Him. It's a hard way to learn a lesson, but it's worth it if we do. Solomon did not repent when the heat was on. God was disappointed, but He did not abandon Solomon during his lifetime because he was David's son. After his death, however, the kingdom of Israel split into two parts. The kings that followed Solomon in both the northern and southern sections were increasingly weak and godless.

KEY LEARNINGS FROM THE STARTER KINGS

I've attempted to pack a lot into this look at the first three kings of Israel. It goes without saying that I've barely touched upon their lengthy and detailed stories. But I think the highlights are enough to identify some key learnings for us to take to heart. Doing this may help us to avoid a fourth quarter fumble in our own lives.

What are those key learnings? I'd like to suggest three spiritual disciplines we should build into our lives. Make them part of your daily worship workout and they'll build muscles of faith that will keep you strong for a lifetime. Here they are:

- Read, respond and rely on God's Word.

- Stay connected with Christians and be accountable.

- Watch your priorities and make sure God is number one.

PLAYING BY THE BOOK
The First Fruits Principle

Saul, David, and Solomon excelled in every way
that matters as long as they kept their eyes on God.
In this busy stressful world, there are
a lot of distractions. We must be careful not
to lose our focus. Here is an activity and
a prayer to help you seek God first.

Worship Workout

Solomon's distractions were self, sex, and silver. What are yours? Being on the offensive for anything that threatens to dethrone God in your life will make a fumble less likely. Take a few minutes to identify three areas you need to work on and write them in the spaces below. (Remember, *anything* that takes your focus off of God can be an idol in your life.)

1. _____

2. _____

3. _____

Priority Prayer

Lord, I confess that I have these areas of weakness, but I want to live all the days of my life Your way—not my own way. I give these areas of weakness to You and open my heart to You now, asking you to guard it with Your Spirit. Help me to make your Word a daily priority. When I search its pages, please open my eyes and ears to the lessons you have for me. Keep me connected to other believers and let me take to heart their efforts to hold me accountable. Finally, Lord, help me to never put more importance on anything than I do on You (even ***good*** things). The only hope I have of finishing life well is staying on Your team, Lord. Thank you for recruiting me. Amen.

But seek first his kingdom and his righteousness, and all these things will be given to you as well. (Matthew 6:33)

FOURTH QUARTER FUMBLES
CHAPTER 2
ASA:
A SAD ENDING TO A STELLAR LIFE

A Costly Error

His name is Bill Buckner and he played baseball for the Los Angeles Dodgers, Chicago Cubs, Boston Red Sox, California Angels, and Kansas City Royals. Although his career spanned more than twenty years and credited him with over 2,700 hits, Bill Buckner is perhaps best remembered for a costly error he committed in the 1986 World Series.

It was Boston Red Sox vs. New York Mets. On October 25, 1986, Boston was leading the series 3 games to 2. In the bottom of the 10th inning the game was tied when Boston moved ahead with a two-run lead. Looking good—but anything can happen in baseball. To prove it, New York battled back to tie the game.

Then Mookie Wilson came up to bat for the Mets, and the tension was electric. After fouling off several pitches, Wilson hit a ground ball straight to Buckner at first base. Imagine Buckner's horror when the ball bounced on the field, rolled under his glove, through his legs and into right field—allowing the winning run for the Mets to score from second base. This forced a 7th game, and the rest is history. The Mets became the 1986 World Champions two nights later.

Overall, 1986 was a stellar season for Bill Buckner. He drove in over 100 runs—including 8 home runs, 22 RBIs and a .340 average in the final month of the season that clinched the pennant for the Red Sox and sent them to the World Series. Yet, one costly error during extra innings in the sixth game became the highlight of Buckner's career that he'd rather forget. (*Wikipedia, the free encyclopedia*; *Wikipedia's* "Bill Buckner" entry)

I f I were a coach, I'd tell you that I have the best team in town!

One of the things I love most about the church where I am lead pastor is that we are a congregation of finishers. My predecessors were tough acts to follow, and I'm grateful to be entrusted with the privilege of carrying forward the spiritual legacy of ministry leaders who finished strong. Our reputation within the community as a church of finishers extends over a period of 146 years, and the entire staff I serve with is committed to preserving that precious legacy of faith. We share the conviction of the apostle Paul, who wrote, "I consider my life nothing to me if only I may finish the race and complete the task the Lord Jesus has given me" (Acts 20:24). To finish as strong as we started, we have to keep on our toes. Being involved in ministry does not mean we are exempt from trials and temptations.

Not long ago, a well-known pastor fumbled big-time. This man was admired, not just by his own congregation of thousands, but by many outside his flock. His ministry was visible and admirable. His light was shining for Christ. Then one day — breaking news! Reports of a sex scandal involving this man hit the media, and his light was snuffed out in a flash. One bold headline in the paper, a lead story on the evening news, and this once mighty man of God tumbled onto the field taking his credibility and his ministry down with him.

The week this story broke, I was listening to a talk radio program. I wavered between being sad and grieved to being downright angry as I heard one caller say, "You know what? That preacher is like that . . . and *all* preachers are like that. I've found that the people who talk most about their faith are usually people who are doing stuff like that behind the scenes." Of course, this is neither fair nor true. Every day, in other arenas, people of high profile are stumbling and fumbling in similar ways. Their indiscretions may get mentioned in passing, if at all. But, when a Christian fumbles like this, people jump on it as an excuse to point their finger and cry "hypocrisy."

Believers are human like everyone else. We are not exempt from temptations. But, as followers of Christ, we are held to a higher standard, and we have the Holy Spirit to help and strengthen us. When we fail to let Him and temptations tackle us, His name is tarnished along with our own. This is why we must always be on guard.

THE FAILURE ADVANTAGE

The Bible is filled with stories about people who let their guard down and fumbled big-time. God has exposed the failures of His people—and not just in a news headline that is "old news" and of no interest after a few days. God immortalized those embarrassing stories in His Word for people to read all throughout history. This makes the Bible utterly unique in the history of world religions. No other book from antiquity talks at length about the failure of its leaders. Instead, they are covered up. You could see this if you studied the sacred literature of the Egyptians, the Babylonians, the Assyrians, and others.

Why does the Bible tell all?

We find the answer in 1 Corinthians 10:6,11, "Now these things occurred as examples, to keep us from setting our hearts on evil things as they did . . . and were written down as warnings for us, on whom the fulfillment of the ages has come." Isn't that good news? As we go through our lives with the Lord, we don't have to learn everything the hard way. It is possible to learn through the examples—both positive and negative—of other people. People like Asa, who had a very strong start in his reign as king of Judah.

IN THE BEGINNING . . . GOD

When Asa came into power, his people were spiritually out of shape. Today we might say that their world view—God's world view—had been corrupted by outside influences. Idolatry and pagan practices from neighboring cultures like the Canaanites had crept into their faith base. In the opening verses of 2 Chronicles 14, we learn that:

> Asa did what was good and right in the eyes of the Lord his God. He removed the foreign altars and the high places, smashed the sacred stones and cut down the Asherah poles. He commanded Judah to seek the Lord the God of their ancestors, and to obey his laws and commands. He removed the high places and incense altars in every town in Judah, and the kingdom was at peace under him. (2 Chronicles 14:2-5)

As you can see, Asa faced a tough game in the beginning. But he took it on, with God as his coach. The bulk of his reign was characterized by reform and revival. The first order of business was to tear down the "high places" that were left over from the Canaanites who were idol worshipers. Biblical scholars are not quite sure exactly what these high places were. Perhaps they were elevated platforms built expressly for the display of idols. Or, they might have been hills or mountains—natural places of higher elevation where they built shrines and altars to false gods. It may have been a combination of the two. Whatever they were, these high places were not pleasing to God. Asa knew this because he knew God's Word. When Moses received the Ten Commandments, the very first one stated in no uncertain terms, "You shall have no other gods before me" (Exodus 20:3). God said it, Asa obeyed it and what happened? Asa's people followed his example and sought God. The kingdom was at peace.

They built and fortified their cities, and it was a prosperous time in Judah's history. Life was good.

TURNAROUND TOUCHDOWN

Then something happened that put Asa's strong leadership to the test. A massive army from Egypt (known then as Cush) came against Judah. Asa's army was vastly outnumbered, and it seemed that there was no hope. Would Asa's reformations stand strong—or fall to ruins? Fortunately, Asa was spiritually prepared for this test. He gathered his army and led them out to face the advancing enemy troops. Then he prayed:

> "Lord, there is no one like you to help the powerless against the mighty. Help us, O Lord our God, for we rely on you, and in your name we have come against this vast army. O Lord, you are our God: do not let man prevail against you." (2 Chronicles 14:11)

When the chips were down, the quality of Asa's faith was tested like gold in the refiner's fire. His dependence on God was true and pure. And what happened? Against all odds, the small nation of Judah defeated the massive Egyptian military.

Would this have happened if Asa had been self-reliant rather than God-reliant? Not a chance. This is a classic example of how God can take an impossible situation and turn it into a glorious victory.

GOING THE EXTRA MILE

So far we've seen that Asa was a good man who depended on God. He was also a man who went the extra mile in seeking the Lord. He had a friend named Azariah, a prophet of the Lord, who came to him and said, "The Lord is with you when you are with him. If you seek him, he will be found by you, but if you forsake him, he will forsake you" (2 Chronicles 15:2).

I love that phrase, "The Lord is with you when you are with him." To me, it says that we need not worry about God being on our side as long as we stay on His side. I have to confess that, earlier in my life, I had a tendency to spend very little time trying to figure out what God wanted me to do in a particular situation. Instead, I would come up with a "great idea" of my own. I'd be in the shower and a lightbulb would go on in my head. I'd grab hold of that idea and start begging God to bless it. Until I was blue in the face I'd plead, "Oh God, bless it, bless it, bless it!" Then one day, wisdom broke through. Wouldn't it be smarter to spend more time front-loading my prayer life and then waiting on God to reveal His idea? Once you figure this out, everything in life comes easier because God is in charge and you can absolutely count on Him to make things happen when He's ready. I like to think of it as floating downstream with the wind at your back rather than in your face. If I spend more time making sure I'm on God's side, then He will naturally bless my efforts—because whatever I do is more likely to come to me by His inspiration than my effort.

Basically, this is what Azariah was telling Asa. "Hey buddy, stick with God, and He'll stick with you. Go your own way, and He'll let you." As Asa took his friend's words to heart, God gave him great ideas and made things happen. Asa stayed strong, did not give up, and his efforts were blessed and rewarded—just as Azariah prophesied (2 Chronicles 15:7).

AZARIAH ALLY

Asa was fortunate to have Azariah to be his spiritual ally and hold him accountable to sticking with God. In fact, because of Azariah's challenge, Asa led Judah in a second round of reforms. In 2 Chronicles 15, there's an impressive list of accomplishments that came about during this time, including the removal of idols from the whole land of Judah, the repair of the altar of the Lord in the Temple, and a huge worship revival. Verse 12 says that, "They entered into a covenant to seek the Lord the God of their fathers, with all their heart and soul." Then, in verse 15, we're told, "They sought God eagerly, and he was found by them. So the Lord gave them rest on every side."

I love the image of people seeking God eagerly. These people didn't have to be dragged to church. Is this what it's like at your house on Sunday morning? When the alarm goes off, do you jump out of bed eagerly and say, "I'm glad to have the chance to go to church?" As you get the kids ready and herd them into the car, is there enthusiastic joy? I know it's a struggle because I have six kids! But you know, I'm their spiritual role model and I need to be an example of eager anticipation as we set out to worship together on Sunday mornings. Honestly, I sometimes don't feel that way. That's when I'm grateful to have my wife Kimberly to be an encouraging ally like Azariah.

Do you have an "Azariah ally" in your life? When you get discouraged and are limping along, is there someone to come alongside you and say, "Hang in there! Don't give up. You're doing a good thing. Stick with God and He will stick with you"? A good place to find a friend like Azariah is in your church. Are you part of a small group, Sunday school class, or support group? During the tough times of life, being connected in this way can make the difference between going the distance with God or lagging behind and even dropping out. It also puts you in a position to be able to encourage someone else who needs an ally like Azariah to help them stick close to God.

TOUGH CHOICES

We've seen that Asa was a good man, a strong leader, and a godly example. Based on all that we know about him, I think we can assume that he was also a family man. But there came a time in his life when he had to make the ultimate tough choice — to put God first, even above his family. Look at the hard thing he did:

> King Asa also disposed of his grandmother Maacah
> from her position as queen mother, because she had
> made a repulsive Asherah pole. (2 Chronicles 15:16)

That's right, Asa fired his grandma! Imagine how hard this must have been for him. However, sometimes in order to keep God first in our lives, we have to take a stand even against people who are closest in our lives — our children, our parents, even our grandparents!

Do you have a friendship or a family relationship that is dragging you down in your effort to follow God? Or, taking this a step further, is there a television show, a hobby, or a pastime that keeps you from wholeheartedly serving God? When this happens, do you make the tough choice Asa did to free yourself from ungodly influences? Or, do you maintain the status quo?

This kind of situation can also happen in businesses or institutions. Did you know that Harvard, Yale, and many other major universities were originally founded to be Bible colleges? Today, they have drifted far from that starting point because they didn't have leaders like Asa who were willing to make the tough choices. Not long ago, the president of my own alma mater actually fired a professor who had changed his position on some key stands regarding God's Word. This was big news! Students protested and this story even made the front page of the Wall Street Journal. Of course, the report made the president look like a fool for his firm stand. But I applaud him because he stood his ground, even though it was hard to do. People and institutions who are willing to make the tough choices are the ones who will keep God's principles alive and strong throughout the generations.

SLIP SLIDING AWAY

We've talked about the highlights of Asa's life. As you can see, he started out strong and continued that way for a very long time. Then, after he had been king for 36 years, there was a subtle change in Asa that ultimately led to a fourth quarter fumble. We see this change recorded in 2 Chronicles 15:17. It says, "Although he did not remove the high places from Israel, Asa's heart was fully committed to the Lord all his life."

In time, Asa, who was so committed to removing idolatry, began to slack off. It's almost like he got tired of being good. These "high places" were like weeds. They kept creeping up. Asa would get rid of them, but the people revived them again and again. After a while, it seems that Asa just grew weary of dealing with them. He probably rationalized this by telling himself, "I had energy when I was younger, but I'm getting too old for this nonsense."

So Asa began to slip slide away. And, in his final years, he made four decisions that caused his life to finish in a slump.

SLEEPING WITH THE ENEMY

Asa's first failure came when Judah was once again facing an enemy. The same man who once depended on God for an impossible victory now turned instead to Ben-Hadad, king of a pagan nation, for help. Asa even took the temple treasure—God's silver and gold—and sent it to Ben-Hadad as a sort of bribe to break a treaty with the nation that threatened Judah in an attempt to force a retreat.

HE "SHOT" THE MESSENGER

God was not pleased! He sent the prophet Hanani to confront Asa with these words:

"Because you relied on the king of Aram and not on
the Lord your God, the army of the king of Aram
has escaped from your hand . . . You have done a
foolish thing and from now on you will be at war." (2
Chronicles 16:7-10)

This was a key moment in Asa's life. He had dropped the ball, and
a friend came to confront him. There was still a chance to recover, if
Asa listened. Instead, he was "angry and enraged." He turned on the
prophet Hanani and had him thrown in prison. As the saying goes,
he shot the messenger. My heart goes out to Asa as I read this story.
Constructive criticism can be a bitter pill to swallow, but it can have
healing value if we heed it. As Asa got older, it seems he lost his
spiritual strength. I think we all have to face this risk as the years
pass. Advancing age predisposes us to think that we've figured life
out. There's an increasing danger of becoming less and less open to
correction. I believe this is what happened to King Asa.

In our church, I always look for opportunities to encourage
our members to "speak the truth in love." I urge them to do this
with each other and also with me and the other pastors on our staff.
As brothers and sisters in Christ, we look out for each other. That
includes pointing out blind spots. But there's another side to that
equation in how truth is received. Someone may love you enough
to warn you about a potential fall they see in your future. When they
confront you, if you become angry and defensive, they may back off
and will not likely respond to you openly again. The angrier your
response, the less likely you will be to receive loving and gentle correction, *and you will be the loser for that.* As scripture says, "Wounds
from a friend can be trusted" (Proverbs 27:6). Our part is to receive
those painful wounds and, in their healing, we will grow.

A BAD SITUATION GETS WORSE

When Asa refused to hear the prophet Hanani's corrective prophecy, his angry response was like an aggressive cancer that spread throughout the kingdom. Hanani's imprisonment was just the first of an epidemic of unjust reactions caused by Asa's own unresolved guilt.

When someone has behaved badly and refused to make amends, have you ever noticed how they sink into a bad mood that just gets worse . . . and worse . . . and worse? I am not a psychologist, but it seems to me that this brooding anger is an attempt to shake off guilt and displace it on someone else. As time passes, the unresolved guilt deepens and so does the outrageous resentment of others. This is precisely what happened to Asa. From a benevolent king he morphed into a ruler who "brutally oppressed some of the people" (2 Corinthians 16:10).

BLIND TO THE LIGHT

People don't always change when they see the light, but sometimes they will take action when they feel the heat. God loves us so much, he'll turn up the heat if that's what it takes to get our attention and help us to change our ways. Unfortunately, Asa forced God's hand. After 39 years as king, God allowed a serious foot disease to afflict Asa. Not all sickness comes as a direct result of sin, but in Asa's case, we are told his affliction was a consequence of his disobedience. Then he compounded his problems by consulting only human physicians and leaving the Lord completely out of his medical protocol (2 Chronicles 16:12-14). And so it came to pass that, after 41 years of a mostly illustrious reign in Judah, Asa died.

The Bible tells us that Asa's body was buried in a tomb he had prepared for himself in Jerusalem and the people "made a huge fire in his honor" (2 Chronicles 16:14). Even though the last few years may have left a bitter impression on his people, the big picture of Asa's life was an honorable one.

Of course, Asa lived before the coming of Jesus. But, as a man who loved God and looked forward to the coming of the Messiah, he was eligible to receive the gift of eternal life. And I believe he did. Looking at the big picture, he leaves behind the story of a life well-lived. But how much better it would have been if he had continued to rely on God rather than other things. Instead, he fumbled and fell, and that makes for a sad ending to a stellar life.

What can we learn from Asa? Let's not forget that he:

- Was a good man.

- Depended on God.

- Went the extra mile in seeking God.

- Was willing to make tough choices.

Could these things be said about you? If so, keep up the good work! You're playing a fine game, but don't forget that *the game's not over until it's over*. Never take your eyes off your Coach and you'll finish strong.

THE END ZONE

There are two springs in the Colorado Rockies, and I'm told they're about thirty or forty feet apart from each other—very close. Yet, because they are on the Continental Divide, one flows west and feeds into the Pacific Ocean. The other, flows east into the Atlantic. Two streams, starting at the same place, yet ending thousands of miles apart. That's the way it is in life. Often, like Asa, we start in one place—the right place. Unless we are careful to stay close to God, we can run off the field and end very far from where we started. Don't let that happen to you.

PLAYING BY THE BOOK
Take Out the Trash

Most of us consider house-keeping to be an important factor in living a healthy, happy life. But *heart*-cleaning is even more important than *house*-cleaning. Here's an exercise to help you identify and discard things that may be cluttering up your heart.

Worship Workout

You may not worship statues or idols, but perhaps there are things you allow to be more of a priority than God in your life. In the space below, write down your "idols." Think prayerfully about this and be honest! Once you've identified the problem areas, ask God to clean them out of your heart. You may even want to write these on a separate piece of paper and literally toss it in the trash as a symbolic act of your personal commitment to clean up your heart.

_____

_____

_____

_____

Now I urge you to take this one step further. Perhaps you already have a friend or family member you can count on to hold you accountable. If so, have a little chat and tell that person how grateful you are to have them as your Azariah Ally. Share with them about the issues you've written on your heart-cleaning list and ask them to tell you if they begin to creep back in. If you don't have someone like that in your life, start praying and keep your eyes open. When your Azariah shows up, don't shoot the messenger!

I am the Lord your God . . . You shall have no other gods before me. (Exodus 20:3)

FOURTH QUARTER FUMBLES

CHAPTER 3

JOASH:
THE BOY KING

Heartbreak Hero

It was Tony Romo's first season as a starter for the Dallas Cowboys, and what a season it was! Tony got his chance and made the most of it. Some even said his stellar performance as a rookie saved the 2007 season for his team.

Tony and the Cowboys headed into the playoffs with high hopes. But Romo was bucking some challenging odds. Since 1979, no NFL quarterback had ever won his first postseason start while playing on the road. But that's another story.

In the final seconds of a hard-fought game, Dallas was trailing Seattle by one point. But Romo had moved his team downfield and into position for an easy field goal. All he had to do was put down that ball and let his teammate Martin Gramatica kick it just 19 yards for a two-point victory. That's when Tony, the newcomer who had saved the season, also ended it for the Dallas Cowboys. Romo fumbled the snap on the field-goal try. With the clock ticking down from 1:19, he had no choice but to run for the end zone. He fell two yards short.

Bottom line: It was a slim 21-20 win for the Seattle Seahawks and a major heartbreak for a young football hero. ("Romo's botched hold grounds Cowboys, lifts Seahawks")

I magine if you woke up tomorrow, turned on the TV to check out the traffic and heard this breaking news:

> *At ten o'clock Eastern Standard Time, Joash Jones*
> *will be sworn in as the next president of the*
> *United States. At the age of seven, Mr. Jones*
> *becomes the youngest president in American history.*

I don't know about you, but I'd do a double take. What? Our *president* — a seven-year old boy? (With three sons of my own, I know what boys are like at that age!) The thought of a small boy as president of the United States — or any country — seems too wild and crazy to fathom. But Judah had a king named Joash who came to the throne at the tender age of seven. No happy, carefree childhood for this little guy! He was thrown into the game early. And, even if he hadn't been so young when he took to the field — well, let's just say that Joash had a very difficult family background. He was playing with a handicap.

PLAYING WITH A HANDICAP

To understand what tough obstacles Joash faced, let me briefly touch on a few historical highlights related to his family tree. (It was a tree loaded down with bad apples.)

Let's start with Joash's grandfather, a man named Jehoram. He was married to Athalia, the daughter of Ahab and Jezebel — perhaps the most infamous couple in biblical history. Cruel, evil, bloodthirsty, idolatrous—these two hardly fit the image of warm and fuzzy Gram and Gramps. For example, during his reign, Grandpa Jehoram murdered his brothers—every last one, and at the end of his life, "He passed away, *to no one's regret*" (2 Chronicles 21:20).

Ahaziah, Joash's father, was next in line. Like father, like son. Nothing much changed until about a year later when Ahaziah was killed and things got even worse. That's when the queen mother Athalia went on a murderous rampage and wiped out the entire royal family of the house of Judah—except for one lone little survivor named Joash. Somehow, Joash's aunt managed to snatch him up and hide him safely away from Athaliah's hit men. Then, after the killing spree was over, Joash was quietly taken to the Temple where he remained for the next six years while Athalia ruled with an iron hand.

WHO'S THE BOSS?

Let's stop for a moment and take a closer look at this story, because there's an important and comforting spiritual lesson we can learn from this action-packed saga. You see, if Joash had not been spared, the line of David in Judah would have been completely wiped out. Athalia may have *thought* she was the one to issue the death sentences, but it was really Satan who was seeking to kill off the family God had chosen to bear the seed of Christ. This was just one of many despicable attempts made by God's enemy to keep the Messiah from coming. For example:

- When the Israelites were in Egypt, Pharoah ordered all the Jewish baby boys killed.

- In the story of Queen Esther, Haman devised a holocaustic plot to exterminate the entire Jewish population in Persia.

- King Herod, unnerved by ancient prophecies and a bright star, sent soldiers to slaughter innocent Israelite babies in Bethlehem.

There were other attempts, as well. But, here's where the wonderful lesson comes in. As we put the pieces of history together, we can see that whenever Satan raised up someone to try to wipe out the line of Christ, God sent someone else to protect and preserve it. For example, in the cases I just mentioned:

- He raised up Jochebed, the courageous mother of Moses. This godly mom hid her son in a basket and planted it strategically to save him and ultimately to liberate the Israelites and lead them to the Promised Land.

- He positioned Queen Esther in the harem of Persia's king and used her in a most remarkable way to expose Haman's plans and then turn them back on him.

- In a dream, He warned Mary and Joseph to take Jesus and flee to Egypt, far away and safe from the slashing swords of Herod's troops.

These are remarkable examples of God's sovereign concern for His children—and His ability to hide them from harm. He did the same for Joash. In his case, Grandma Athalia's evil intentions backfired altogether. You see, while he was hidden away in the temple, Joash was being trained in the ways of God by a righteous priest named Jehoida. As Joash learned God's Word, the seeds of true faith, hope and revival were planted in this child's heart. Ultimately, through his kingship, this resulted in breaking the cycle of evil in Judah that had been perpetuated through Joash's bad apple family.

God is sovereign. *He's* the Boss! His plans cannot and will not be thwarted. He helped Joash overcome the most difficult family background imaginable, and He can help you with whatever difficult obstacle you are facing today.

FOLLOW THE RIGHT LEADER

Now we come full circle, back to the coronation of the seven-year-old boy king, Joash. Imagine how he must have felt, so little and innocent, as the priest "brought the prince into view, crowned him, handed him the scroll of God's covenant and made him king. As Jehoida and his sons anointed him they shouted, 'Long live the king!'" (2 Chronicles 23:11, The Message).

This was the beginning of Joash's forty-year reign in Jerusalem. And, for the most part, they were good years. The Bible says that "Joash did what was right in the eyes of the Lord all the years of Jehoida the priest." While he may have had the worst possible parents, he had a godly guardian to guide him. Following the right leader, the boy king grew to be a man king. And a good one, too!

Here is another comforting lesson for us to learn from the story of Joash. Usually our spiritual role models are our parents. That is always God's Plan A. In Ephesians 6:1-3, it says: "Children, obey your parents in the Lord, for this is right. 'Honor your father and mother . . . that it may go well with you and that you may enjoy long life on the earth.'"

If you have been blessed with godly parents, you are fortunate indeed. May you continue to honor them throughout your life so that you will have the wind at your back from start to finish. But perhaps, like Joash, you have lacked the guidance of Christian parents. Maybe you feel your spiritual growth has been stunted. If so, God has a Plan B. As He did for Joash, He can provide a mentor to disciple you in His ways. Ask Him to do that, and He will. Then, please . . .

Remember your leaders, who spoke the word of God
to you. Consider the outcome of their way of life and
imitate their faith. (Hebrews 13:7)

It's never too late to start following God's chosen leaders. Get
behind them and they won't lead you astray.

A PURPOSE DRIVEN LIFE

Joash got behind the right leader. The priest, Jehoida, not only
helped him to grow up, but also to find his purpose in life. *One* of
the keys to living a successful and fulfilling life is to find the special
assignment God has for you. There are many good things you can
and will do throughout your lifetime. But, they may not be the things
God wants you to do. I believe God has a unique mission for you, as
He does for each of His children—two or three things that He had in
mind when He created you. Early on, Joash knew what his special
assignment was—probably because of the strong spiritual guidance
he received from Jehoida. Joash was called and privileged to be the
one God used to restore the Temple in Jerusalem, which had suffered
abominable neglect during the rule of Joash's predecessors.

When Joash was convicted about his God-given purpose in life,
he felt an urgent need to get on with the project. So, he called together
the priests and Levites and directed them to collect the tax imposed
by Moses. To his surprise, the priests didn't seem to share his zeal for
restoring the Temple. They dragged their feet. What would happen
if you were in charge of this project? Many people would lose their
enthusiasm and pass the buck, blaming the committee members who
didn't do their share. But Joash had a plan, and you can read about it
in 2 Chronicles 24:8-13. Here are a few highlights from that passage:

A chest was made and placed outside at the gate of the
temple of the Lord . . . and all the people brought their

contributions gladly, dropping them into the chest until it was full. Whenever the chest was brought in by the Levites to the king's officials and they saw that there was a large amount of money . . . the king and Jehoida gave it to the men who carried out the work required for the temple of the Lord . . . The men in charge of the work were diligent, and the repairs progressed under them. They rebuilt the temple of God according to the original design and reinforced it.

Joash came up with a plan that inspired others to give. It became a church project and brought people together. Even today, the *Joash Chest* is an old-fashioned term for an offering box. We have one in the lobby of our church.

SINK OR SWIM?

We've taken a look at Joash's life and seen how incredibly gracious God was to this man who started out with a lot going against him. If he could suddenly reappear today, I'm pretty sure he'd say "Amen!" to that. And, he would undoubtedly list his priestly mentor Jehoida as the one who helped him play to win for a long, long time. All throughout his childhood and well into his adulthood, Joash leaned on faithful Jehoida. But finally the time came when God wanted Joash to stand on his own two feet. That time came when Jehoida was "old and full of years, and he died at the age of a hundred and thirty" (2 Chronicles 24:15).

Suddenly, Joash was forced to sink or swim! And, I'm sorry to say that he began to go down. All of those years, he had drawn strength from Jehoida's faith, but he had never developed a strong faith of his own. This might have been an event that brought out the best in Joash — like the rain that causes a seedling to grow into a strong plant. But because the spiritual seeds had never put down roots, Joash's faith was washed away in the storm.

Are you a leaner like Joash? Or a leader like Jehoida? There is a time for being mentored and discipled, but the goal God always has for us is to become a mentor and discipler to others. As it says in Hebrews 5:13-14:

> Anyone who lives on milk, being still an infant, is not acquainted with the teaching about righteousness. But solid food is for the mature, who by constant use have trained themselves to distinguish good from evil.

A FINICKY LISTENER

Leaner or not, Joash didn't have to come tumbling down after Jehoida died. He could have confessed his weakness to God and looked for new spiritual counsel to help him develop his own muscles of faith, but he didn't.

I have a theory that has developed as I've watched Christians grow. I call it the Finicky Listener theory, and it goes something like this: Whatever style of teaching or worship a person was raised on when they first came to Christ becomes the model they insist and fixate on as they grow. Many people are finicky leaders and listeners. This is not such a good thing, because it limits God and can, if carried to an extreme, stunt our Christian growth. You see, as God takes us from faith to faith, He may want to use a teacher who has a different style of teaching. He knows we can get stuck in a rut and, to push us through, He may want to expose us to something fresh, new and unique. Although God has parameters and boundaries we must observe (we can't just do our own thing), He does not have a rigid checklist of worship mandatories. Pastors and Bible Study leaders are not like identically shaped cookies from the same cutter. And neither are people. For example, the younger generation in our church usually prefer a contemporary style of worship with a praise band and worship leaders. Others in our congregation were raised on the classic hymns that have come down through the ages and a more traditional and structured order of worship. So, we have services geared towards each of these preferences—designed and measured, of course, by the non-negotiable truths of God's Word.

Now it is true confession time. Yes, I was once a finicky listener. Back in the 1960s, I came to Christ at West End Presbyterian Church in Hopewell, Virginia. My pastor was a man named Kennedy Smart. He was my hero, and I measured every other preacher and teacher against him. For years, worship had to be just like it was at West End Presbyterian or it wasn't worship as far as I was concerned. Eventually, though, I learned that we miss out when we are finicky listeners. And that God gives us variety in order to make us into more versatile and vibrant reflectors of His own character. It's a shame that so many people build their faith around a culture just because it is comfortable and familiar to them. Instead, we should build our faith around the principles of God's Word that are always the same "yesterday, today and forever" (Hebrews 13:8).

After Jehoida died, Joash stopped building altogether. He clung to what he knew and refused to proactively seek new and fresh spiritual encouragement to replace what he had lost. This was a vulnerable time in his life, and Satan took advantage of it as you'll soon see. We can learn from Joash's experience by being aware that times will come that will push us out of our comfort zone. Going away to college, moving to a new state, the loss of a loved one. When something happens to stir the waters, "let us not give up . . . as some are in the habit of doing, but let us encourage one another..." (Hebrews 10:25).

THE HEAT IS ON

As we've seen, Joash fumbled spiritually following the death of Jehoida. He fumbled again when the "officials of Judah came and paid homage." During this summit meeting, suggestions were made. Advice was given. And, the Bible says that Joash listened without discernment.

As a result, "they abandoned the temple of the Lord, the God of their fathers, and worshiped Asherah poles" (2 Chronicles 24:17-19).

What a tragic situation this was. The good growth that had taken place in Judah because of Joash's early commitment was crumbling because he could not stand up against the pressure of his political peers. And the story gets worse and worse. God, who is always just, sent Jehoida's son, Zechariah, to confront Joash in love. These two men probably played together when they were growing up. In essence, they had been raised by the same dad. They were surely like brothers in many ways. Zechariah tried to warn Joash by saying:

> This is what God says: "Why do you disobey the Lord's commands? You will not prosper. Because you have forsaken the Lord, he has forsaken you." (2 Chronicles 24:20)

These are pretty strong words, but did they jerk Joash to his senses? Did he heed this righteous warning and run to God for forgiveness and restoration? Did he stand up and use whatever remaining time he had left as king to protect and preserve his legacy as a godly ruler? I think you know the answer is "no." Not only did Joash turn a deaf ear towards Zechariah, he turned against him and had him stoned to death in the courtyard of the temple.

I hope there will never be a time in your walk when God finds it necessary to send someone like Zechariah to speak the truth in love. But, if He does, I pray you will receive the truth in love. It may mean the difference between a strong victory or, as in Joash's case, a disappointing tragedy.

FOURTH QUARTER PENALTY

That tragedy came in the 40th year of Joash's reign. The boy king had become a man, but he was not an old man. At 47, he may have thought he had many more years to repair the damage done by his fumbles in the years after Jehoida died. If he did, he was wrong. His life was cut short in a violent and unexpected way. Here's the story, recorded in 2 Chronicles 24:23-25:

> At the turn of the year, the army of Aram marched against Joash; it invaded Judah and Jerusalem and killed all the leaders of the people. They sent all the plunder to their king in Damascus. Although the Aramean army had come with only a few men, the Lord delivered into their hands a much larger army. Because Judah had forsaken the Lord, the God of their fathers, they left Joash severely wounded. His officials conspired against him for murdering the son of Jehoida the priest, and they killed him in his bed.

I have included this lengthy passage from the Bible, because it's important to see that our actions not only impact our lives, but also the lives of others. Joash's spiritual neglect and deliberate disobedience of God's guidelines was a setback for himself and the entire nation of Judah. And when God's judgment fell, everyone was penalized—just as an entire football team is pushed back away from the goal when a player commits a personal foul.

I know this story ends on a sad note, but there is a glimmer of hope—as there always is with God. Because of His amazing grace, and because of the way He protected and pursued Joash in his early years, I believe the door of Heaven opened to this man when he took his last earthly breath. He made serious mistakes, but I think he had a heart that was tender towards God and a vision that looked forward to the promised Savior.

It may be a stretch, but I even see a symbolic ray of light in the "wrap" of Joash's life that is recorded in 2 Chronicles 24:25. It says, "So he died and was buried in the City of David, but not in the tomb of the kings." When Joash's life was over, he left behind the kingdom of earth and moved to the Holy City where David's heir Jesus is king. Although it is always God's plan for us to start and finish well, He knows our human weakness. And, He's able and willing to recover the ball for us when we fumble.

PLAYING BY THE BOOK

Preventative Measures

Joash's reign ended disastrously because he neglected to cultivate a strong faith of his own. The best way to ensure that this doesn't happen in your life is to deliberately cultivate good spiritual habits. Here are some suggestions to help you stay in shape.

Worship Workout

God's Word is our spiritual *food*. And prayer opens the conduit that allows us to drink daily of the Living Water through a personal connection to God. Here is a practical suggestion for cultivating the habit of *feeding* on God's Word and *drinking* in His Spirit. Think of this page as an appointment card. Write below a time and place where you commit to meet with God each day for your worship workout. Or, why not actually log that time into your personal or business planner? Taking that appointment as seriously as any other in your book will change your life!

Subject: Standing Appointment with God!

Time: _____

Place:_____

Agenda: Bible study and prayer time

Do not merely listen to the word of God, and so deceive yourselves. Do what it says. (James 1:22)

FOURTH QUARTER FUMBLES

CHAPTER 4

JEHOSHAPHAT:
The Lord Judges

Famous Last Words

Many a fine athlete has lived to regret those famous last words, "There's no way we can lose this game." On April 5, 1993, Chris Webber joined the ranks. That was the day his team, the Michigan Wolverines battled the University of North Carolina Tar Heels in the NCAA championship basketball game.

With 11 seconds left on the clock, it was a close game when Webber, realizing he was in a tight spot, was grasping for a way out. On an impulse, he brought his hands together to form a "T" for timeout. Only problem was, the Wolverines had used their last timeout only minutes before.

From the bench, Webber's teammates raised a united cry to remind him, "No! No timeouts! No timeouts." But with the din of the excited crowd, Webber thought they were agreeing with his call. The result? A technical foul on Michigan that brought Tar Heels player Donald Williams to the line. Williams sank both free throws and stretched UNC's lead to a comfortable advantage. As the clock ran out, the defeated Wolverines stood frozen in disbelief. With a sudden realization of what had happened, Webber turned pale. In a few split seconds, his earlier vote of confidence melted away into famous last words. And with tears in his eyes, the falling star now cried out, "I cost our team the game." ("Webber's timeout hands title to Carolina")

READ ALL ABOUT IT:

2 Chronicles 17-20.

C hoosing a child's name is a very serious matter. After all, the name we are given at birth determines our official identity for the rest of our lives—and even beyond.

When a baby is on the way, excited parents spend hours of time thinking and talking about what their little one will be called. As a parent, I remember that feeling of serendipity—when we suddenly hit upon just the right name for each of our children.

Often as we read about people in the Bible, we learn that their names had a prophetic significance that pointed towards their God-given destiny. In this chapter, we're going to be looking at the life of Jehoshaphat—a man whose name in Hebrew means, "the Lord judges."

As you'll see, good judgment and a high regard for justice were qualities that stood out in Jehoshaphat's character and also shaped his leadership style. In the beginning of his reign, Jehoshaphat was a strong king who strove towards righteousness, not only for himself but also for his people. However, later in his life there were a few times when a weakness in his human nature interfered with his good judgment. Before we examine his fourth quarter fumbles, let's take a look at Jehoshaphat's early strengths because they were really quite commendable.

STARTING STRONG

From a very early age, Jehoshaphat learned to judge rightly between the ways of the Lord and the ways of the world. In 2

Chronicles 17:4-6, it says that he "sought the God of his father and followed his commands rather than the practices of Israel. The Lord established the kingdom under his control . . .*His heart was devoted to the ways of the Lord*; furthermore, he removed the high places and the Asherah poles from Judah."

You may be confused by the first part of this passage unless you recall that the twelve tribes of Israel had split into two distinct groups. The ten northern tribes retained the name of Israel, while the two southern tribes became Judah. Jehoshaphat succeeded his father, Asa, as king of Judah in the south.

As you may recall, Asa was a man who "walked the talk" for most of his life. So his son Jehoshaphat had the benefit of a godly upbringing. He grew up to be a devoted man of God with a solid foundation of faith, despite the corruption of idolatry that was gaining ground in neighboring nations. Young, energetic, and on fire, Jehoshaphat's charismatic faith drew his people like a magnet. This was a time of great spiritual revival in the land of Judah, and it didn't just happen by accident. Jehoshaphat was a great organizer, and he implemented a plan to make sure that Judah was a "nation under God."

TEACHING THE WORD

One of the most noteworthy accomplishments in Jehoshaphat's record was his attention to making sure that the Word of God was taught all throughout Judah. He did this by selecting a group of more than a dozen "professors" who went out to educate the people in the ways of the Lord. In 2 Chronicles 7:7-9 it says: "taking with them the Book of the Law of the Lord; they went around to all the towns of Judah and taught the people." These teachers did not just make random visits as guest speakers in select synagogues. They were responsible for ongoing training programs within their assigned territories. This was Scripture 101: Applying God's Word to Life. And it was one of the greatest contributions Jehoshaphat made during his 25 years as king in Judah.

JUSTICE FOR ALL

Another achievement was to establish God's holy law as the legal rule book for the entire kingdom. True to his name, Jehoshaphat elevated justice and fairness to the highest priority. He was committed to making sure that God was the judge in every matter that arose. In 2 Chronicles 19, you'll find a detailed account of Jehoshaphat's legal plan, but let me just lift out a few of the details for you here.

First of all, Jehoshaphat was an evangelical king. On a regular basis, he left his headquarters in Jerusalem and went out among the people to urge them to turn to the Lord. He took it seriously that "the buck stops here" and personally traveled from town to town, challenging the people to respond to God. His own commitment was a personal example they could see and follow.

Next, King Jehoshaphat appointed judges to live among the people in the fortified cities of Judah. When he couldn't be there himself, these officials were God's legal, moral, and spiritual representatives. And he sternly commissioned them to represent Him well. In verse 6 of 2 Chronicles 19, it says that he told them, "Consider carefully what you do, because you are not judging for man but for the Lord, who is with you whenever you give a verdict." Furthermore, in verse 7, Jehoshaphat warned these officials to, "Judge carefully, for with the Lord our God there is no injustice or partiality or bribery." What wise leadership these judges had from their king! I am sure there was a quality control system in place to hold them accountable to the important responsibility entrusted to them.

A SONG AND A PRAYER

As you can see, Jehoshaphat had many godly traits that made him a strong leader. But his greatest strength of all surely came from his attention to worship.

An example of this—and one of the most amazing stories in the Bible—is found in 2 Chronicles 20. Here is an account of how Jehoshaphat's faith was put to the supreme test when a vast army came to make war on Judah. The number of troops marching towards Jerusalem was staggering. Little Judah was outnumbered and out of her league, and doom appeared imminent. (For all you fellow football fans, think Green Bay Packers vs. Mayberry Musketeers!)

As king, Jehoshaphat faced more than a massive army in this desperate situation. This was a watershed moment—both in his career and his life. It was the moment when God put his faith to the test to see if it really had muscle. I can only imagine how he felt when he received this report from his scouts: "A huge force is on its way from beyond the Dead Sea to fight you. There's no time to waste" (2 Chronicles 20:1-2, The Message).

No time to waste. At this point, it might seem best to hoist up a white flag and surrender. But what do you think Jehoshaphat did? Call out the troops? Activate the National Guard? The Bible tells us that he was alarmed. But instead of giving into panic, he did what all of us *should* do in an emergency—even though most of us don't.

Like a coach who just lost his quarterback, Jehoshaphat called his team together for a spiritual huddle. From the youngest to the oldest, the people of Judah came pouring into Jerusalem and gathered in the courtyard of the temple. Then, their king came out to meet them, and led them in this inspiring prayer:

"Lord, the God of our ancestors, are you not the God who is in heaven? You rule over all the kingdoms of the nations. Power and might are in your hand, and no one can withstand you...Our God, will you not judge them? For we have no power to face this vast army that is attacking us. *We do not know what to do, but our eyes are upon you.*" (2 Chronicles 20: 6,12)

I love to think about this scene! Dads and moms standing with their little children, heads bowed, resting in a supernatural peace that fell upon them as their king prayed with trust and faith in Almighty God. Despite their human helplessness, they did not fall apart. Instead, they looked together towards their one and only Hope. And something amazing happened. A man named Jahaziel stood up in the assembly. Filled with the Spirit of God, he said:

Listen, King Jehoshaphat and all who live in Judah and Jerusalem! This is what the Lord says to you: "Do not be afraid or discouraged because of this vast army. For the battle is not yours, but God's." (2 Chronicles 20:15)

Believe it or not, this story gets even better! Early the next morning, Jehoshaphat dispatched his troops to go out and meet the advancing enemy. From a human perspective, they remained out-numbered. They were still out of their league. But they had a secret weapon and Jehoshaphat reminded them about it as they went onto the battlefield. Here's how the Bible story goes:

As they set out, Jehoshaphat stood and said, "Listen to me, Judah and people of Jerusalem! Have faith in the Lord your God and you will be upheld; have faith in his prophets and you will be successful." After

> consulting the people, Jehoshaphat appointed men to sing to the Lord and to praise him for the splendor of his holiness as they went out at the head of the army, saying: "Give thanks to the Lord, for his love endures forever." As they began to sing and praise, the Lord sent ambushes against the men of Ammon and Moab and Mount Seir who were invading Judah, and they were defeated. (2 Chronicles 20:20-22)

That's the story of how a vast army was put down with a prayer and a song. A prayer of faith. A song of praise. A radical strategy, but it worked—because it was God's strategy, not man's.

This is a great story. (Wouldn't it make an exciting movie?) And the greatest thing about it is that it's true—and we can learn something from it that will make a big difference as we fight our own battles in life. So, before we move on, let me ask you a question. What vast army are *you* facing today? Maybe you are overwhelmed by financial problems. Perhaps you've gotten bad news about your health or the health of someone you love. Could it be that the enemy Satan is threatening to destroy your marriage and tear your home apart? You've got a choice regarding how you face that "army" in your life. You can stew and worry or spin your wheels. You can devise some sort of strategy of your own to fight the battle. Or, like Jehoshaphat, you can resolve to inquire of the Lord and trust His coaching—even when it seems contrary to human logic.

You can also remember that you are not alone. As a child of God, you have brothers and sisters in Christ to support you in prayer and to come alongside you. If you have a church family, you know what I'm talking about. If not, isn't it time you found one? I can tell you from my own experience that when I walk into our church on Sunday morning and see our congregation all around me, my problems seem this big—and God seems *THIS BIG*. As we worship together and study the Word, all the disturbing headlines on the news and the troubles I face in my own life are put into perspective against the sovereign power of my Father God.

Every week, when I work with our worship pastor and his team to plan our services, we always remind each other to make sure we give highest priority to the "two W's"—Worship and the Word. Through his example, this was the legacy Jehoshaphat left for his family, his nation, and even for us. I wish I could end the story here and say that he lived happily ever after. Unfortunately, as I mentioned in the opening of this chapter, Jehoshaphat made a few poor judgment calls that left a mark on his otherwise shining legacy. Let's take a look at those now.

GUILT BY ASSOCIATION

Long before the "fourth quarter" of his life, Jehoshaphat had a weak tendency that he should have dealt with, but didn't. Like so many young Christians today, he thought he could mingle with the world without jeopardizing his own spiritual strength. As a result of this erroneous thinking, Jehoshaphat had a bad habit of getting involved with the wrong people. Unfortunately, this weakness crept in when he chose to "ally himself with Ahab by marriage" (2 Chronicles 18:1). Let me remind you that Ahab and Jezebel were rulers in the northern kingdom of Israel. When Jehoshaphat married their daughter, these two powerful and notoriously evil people became his in-laws. You've heard the expression "a match made in heaven." Well, Jehoshaphat's marriage was "a match made in hell." To give you a modern frame of reference, it would be like Billy Graham choosing to ally himself in marriage with a notorious ISIS terrorist—that bad. With this poor alliance came very serious consequences—not just for Jehoshaphat, but for his entire nation. You see, because of this, Judah became involved in a war they had no business being part of. As Ahab's son-in-law, Jehoshaphat was caught between a rock and a hard place when Ahab asked him, "Will you go with me against Ramoth Gilead?" (2 Chronicles 3:4).

To his credit, Jehoshaphat did try to convince Ahab to seek God's will by consulting the prophets. This just turned out to be a joke since Israel was entrenched in idolatry at this time and the prophets Ahab consulted were prophets of Baal.

Again, Jehoshaphat tried to steer his father-in-law in the right direction by saying, "Is there not a prophet of the Lord here whom we can inquire of?" (2 Chronicles 3:6).

Imagine his consternation when he got this reply from Ahab: "There is still one man through whom we can inquire of the Lord, but I hate him because he never prophesies anything good about me, but always bad" (2 Chronicles 3:7).

Are you getting the picture? Jehoshaphat was learning too late that he had married into a family that had no respect for God. Despite his devotion to the Lord and his commitment to righteousness as leader of Judah, he was now involved in a war where God was not even consulted.

Have you ever been in a situation like this? It's really challenging to be *in the world* but not *of the world*. When the people closest to us do not share our commitment to God, our lives can careen out of control very easily. In Jehoshaphat's case, I'm sure he rationalized to himself that marrying Ahab's daughter was a good political move. He undoubtedly wanted to develop good diplomatic relations with the ten northern tribes but, by marrying into this family, he contradicted his own spiritual convictions. And when a serious crisis arose, he and his nation were in a very compromising situation. This was Ahab's war and he was making the calls. Even though Jehoshaphat tried to be a witness, he failed.

There is a Japanese proverb that goes something like this. "When the character of a man is not clear to you, look at his friends." Despite his own righteous character, Jehoshaphat was not discerning about his friendships and alliances. By seeing how seriously this impacted his walk, perhaps we can safeguard our own. Is there a red flag going up in your mind right now? What is it for you? A friend who may lead you down a path where you are guilty by association? Or, perhaps something else. A television program, movies or books that corrupt your Christian world view. Even something that might seem good like your computer or a hobby that gradually takes over your time and knocks God off His rightful place as first in your life.

I urge you to give careful thought and prayer to this. You may have to make a difficult choice to walk away from someone or something in your life, but in the long run you'll save yourself from a sad spiritual fumble.

DON'T JUST LISTEN . . . *HEAR!*

Let's go back to the scene we just looked at. Remember that Ahab said he didn't want to call for the one prophet of the Lord in his kingdom. Why? Because he didn't want to hear what he had to say. But apparently Jehoshaphat insisted and so a messenger was sent to summon Micaiah, the prophet.

If you ever doubted that God has a sense of humor, turn to 2 Chronicles 18:12-22. The account of Ahab's meeting with Micaiah will give you a good laugh. Let me highlight that story here, using selected verses from *The Message,* a contemporary paraphrase of the Bible.

Before Micaiah even gets to the court, Ahab's messenger has briefed him on what's up. He says:

"The prophets have all said *Yes* to the king. Make it unanimous— vote Yes!"

In reply, Micaiah insists, "As sure as God lives, what

God says, I'll say."

When Micaiah arrives in court, it's clear to him that Ahab has already made up his mind what he's going to do. Nothing he says is going to make a difference, so when Ahab asks him what to do, he says "Go ahead."

Here's where it gets a little bit funny. Ahab is suspicious of this answer—as if he knows it's the wrong one. He says to Micaiah:

> "Not so fast . . . How many times have I made you promise under oath to tell me the truth and nothing but the truth?"

So Micaiah tells him that God has filled the mouths of his prophets with lies. "God has pronounced your doom," he says, only to be sent off to jail by a very ticked-off King Ahab. So what does all of this have to do with Jehoshaphat, who made such a strong start in his commitment to teach God's truth throughout his nation? Well, in this story, Jehoshaphat stands by. He listens, but he doesn't hear. And so, when Ahab decides to go ahead and do battle with the enemy, Jehoshaphat is dragged into the fight.

A GULLIBLE GUY WHO LIVED TO REGRET IT

Now the story gets even sadder, because not only does Jehoshaphat stand by in silence, he becomes the victim of a deadly scam. You see, as the two kings go off together to Ramoth Gilead, Ahab convinces Jehoshaphat to switch royal robes so they can enter the battle disguised. Of course, the only one who would benefit from this plan is Ahab—because the enemy warriors obviously would be looking for him on that battlefield, with orders to kill. What was Jehoshaphat thinking when he agreed to do this? Perhaps he thought, "This is my father-in-law. He wouldn't put me in jeopardy." But this is exactly what Ahab did.

I have to admit that my heart goes out to Jehoshaphat. On occasion, I've fallen into the trap of being gullible with people I assume I can trust. Usually when this happens to me, I'm the brunt of a good-natured joke spearheaded by a friend or one of my ministry partners. It's all in good fun. But, Ahab's intentions towards Jehoshaphat were neither good, nor fun. He was hoping to protect himself by letting his own son-in-law take a deadly hit. Fortunately, God was watching over His gullible child and protected him. Jehoshaphat lived through this close call, but he most certainly lived to regret it.

HISTORY REPEATS ITSELF

I'd like to say that Jehoshaphat learned from this close call. Sadly, though, there were other times later in his life when he made poor alliances until, finally, God's grace wore thin. After one particular time when he joined forces with Ahaziah (Ahab's successor), God sent a prophet to Jehoshaphat with this sad news. "Because you have made an alliance with Ahaziah, the Lord will destroy what you have made" (2 Chronicles 20:37).

The next verse in the Bible tells of Jehoshaphat's death and burial in Jerusalem. It's a sad ending to a story with so many happy highlights. Because of God's great mercy, it's a story that has been preserved in the Bible for us to learn from. Despite his fumbles, the legacy of King Jehoshaphat is a testimony to the meaning of his name. The Lord judged his life worthy to be immortalized in His Word. If we imitate his strengths and learn from his weaknesses, we can finish our own life victoriously.

PLAYING BY THE BOOK

Fight your battles with a prayer and a song

When a huge army came against Jehoshaphat, a prayer and a song were the only weapons he needed to defeat the enemy. Yet, he almost forfeited his life at Ramoth-Gilead because he lost his spiritual focus. Here's a way you can remind yourself to keep your eyes upon Jesus as you face life's battles, great and small.

Worship Workout

Take a 3 x 5 note card or a small piece of paper. On one side, in big bold letters, use the guideline below to write a note to yourself. Be sure to record your name in the first blank and a description of your personal "vast army" in the second:

"_____, do not be afraid or discouraged because of this vast army _____
_____. For the battle is not yours, but God's." (2 Chronicles 20:15)

Below that, write this prayer from scripture:

O Lord, I come to you now and give you this battle. I do not know what to do, but my eyes are upon You. (2 Chronicles 10:12)

Flip your card over now and write the lyrics of your favorite hymn or praise song. Choose a song that moves your heart and helps lift you into the arms of your Savior. Here's one of my favorites:

Turn your eyes upon Jesus,
Look full in His wonderful face;
And the things of earth will grow strangely dim
In the light of His glory and grace.
(Helen Howarth Lemmel)

This is your battle card. Carry it in your planner, your purse or your pocket. Or, if you prefer, display it on your refrigerator or bathroom mirror. Whenever you feel like Satan is sending a vast army against you, take up your weapons and remember how God gave Jehoshaphat victory in response to a prayer and a song.

You will keep in perfect peace him whose mind is steadfast, because he trusts in you. (Isaiah 26:3)

FOURTH QUARTER FUMBLES

CHAPTER 5

AMAZIAH:
The Half-Hearted Hero

It's not over 'til it's over

Olympic snowboarder Lindsey Jacobellis was going for the gold. And she nearly had it. In fact, she was so close she could practically have crawled across the finish line and claimed her medal. That's when it happened.

Lindsey was on the home stretch to a runaway victory when she attempted something called the "backside method grab." A tricky 60-degree twist in front of the grandstand—a move that that some would later call "hot-dogging." Jacobellis challenged that accusation, insisting that she was following a standard strategy—finishing with style and flair. After all, that's a big part of what snowboarding is all about. In the end, it really didn't matter. So close to her goal (and the gold), Lindsey Jacobellis went tumbling out of bounds, just shy of the finish line. When it was over . . . it was *really* over. ("Jacobellis loses shot at gold with stumble")

READ ALL ABOUT IT:

2 Chronicles 25

W hen you hear the word "hero," who do you think of?

Maybe it's someone close to you who has played an important role in shaping your life—a parent, a teacher or a mentor who exemplifies all you would like to be. Perhaps it's someone you have admired from a distance. Someone in the public eye who has performed a courageous or selfless act—a soldier, a firefighter, a police officer, a generous philanthropist. We all have our heroes.

I think God might define a hero as someone who is wholeheartedly committed to Him, from start to finish. Think about the heroes of the Bible like Abraham, Moses, Mary and Joseph, Peter and Paul . . . Jesus. Only one person on this list lived a perfect life. The others were people like you and me who had faults and frailties. But there was one trait they had in common that pleased God. That trait was their wholehearted commitment to Him.

In this chapter, we're going to look at the life of King Amaziah. In his day, he was probably looked up to as a hero by little boys growing up in Judah and by their parents and other people who welcomed the positive contributions he made to their society. Before we're even told what those contributions were in 2 Chronicles 25, we learn that, by God's standards, this man fell short of being a hero. Amaziah's story begins with this description:

> Amaziah was twenty-five years old when he became
> king, and he reigned in Jerusalem twenty-nine years
> . . . He did what was right in the eyes of the Lord, *but*
> *not wholeheartedly*. (2 Chronicles 25:1-2)

From the start, Amaziah had a spiritual handicap that predisposed him to fumble. The way this is written reminds me of that old saying that a half-truth is really a lie. Half a heart is really no heart when the chips are down, as you'll see. But first, let's take a look at Amaziah's beginning and the good things he accomplished before God was compelled to teach him a lesson the hard way.

RIGHTEOUS REVENGE

Amaziah came to the throne following the assassination of his father, Joash. The kingdom of Judah was in turmoil, and I'm sure there was great political strife. Much of this was due to the spiritual mistakes Joash made toward the end of his reign. These experiences certainly should have been a red flag to Amaziah. You would think that he would have looked back and carefully examined what his father Joash did right and also what he did wrong. He could have learned from Joash's mistakes, as well as from his godly example.

In any case, this was a time of crisis in Judah, and Amaziah was a young man. In light of what he had to deal with, he displayed wisdom by waiting to take action against his father's murderers until "after the kingdom was firmly in his control" (2 Chronicles 25:3). He didn't just jump in and go after the perpetrators. But after things stabilized, under the guidelines of the law of Moses, Amaziah finally did round up the officials who murdered his dad and had them executed. The Bible says he did not kill the sons of those officials because God's law stated that each person was to pay for their own sins. To his credit, Amaziah followed God's directions in this whole process of serving justice.

The execution of Joash's assassins was a true case of righteous revenge. I know that some people get hung up reading parts of the Old Testament that describe killing and violence as being within God's will. We love to think of God as our compassionate and tenderhearted Father, but we are not so comfortable with His furious judgment. That's a subject that could fill another book, and I don't want to go off on a tangent about it here. Let me just say, though, that in order to be the sovereign and flawless God that He is, our Lord must be *perfectly righteous* as well as *perfectly loving*.

If you are prone to wrestling with passages in the Old Testament that seem to present God in a harsh light, perhaps it will help if you remember that He was preparing a way for Jesus to come into the world and redeem our sins to save us from *eternal* judgment. At the same time, Satan was doing everything he could to prevent that from happening. There was (and still is) a greater battle going on — a spiritual war, with Satan and his troops on the offensive. Think of God's defense of His family by asking what you would do if someone invaded your home and hurt or killed the people who are dearest to you.

There are always casualties in warfare, but death and suffering were never God's choice. His original plan for mankind included safety and protection, but it also required human submission to His divine will. This is not so different than the "house rules" we make for our families, is it? When our ancestors Adam and Eve chose not to submit to God's house rules, *they also chose death* for themselves — and for the rest of us. It was not God's choice. It was theirs. The necessity for judgment came as a consequence to their self-will. From that point on God could have disowned his human children — but He didn't! Instead He made a plan to come and retrieve us because we could not make it back to Him on our own. He clothed Himself in a human body, came to earth as Jesus and said, "I'll take your licks. I love you enough to die for you." What more could God do to show us that He's absolutely crazy about us?

BIGGER IS NOT ALWAYS BETTER (OR BLESSED)

Now, let's get back to Amaziah. With order restored and justice served for the murder of his father, the king now turned his attention to protecting his people. Another battle was on the horizon with Judah's neighbor Edom. Amaziah wanted his country to be ready, so he organized a strong military with 300,000 young soldiers—men who were "ready for military service, able to handle the spear and the shield." (2 Chronicles 25:6)

So far, so good! Amaziah was running toward the goal. Then he made a strategic error. He decided that his military was not big enough and hired 100,000 soldiers from the northern kingdom of Israel to join his army. God was not pleased. He sent a prophet to deliver this message:

> "O king, these troops from Israel must not march with
> you, for the Lord is not with Israel . . . Even if you go
> and fight courageously in battle, God will overthrow
> you before the enemy, for God has the power to help
> or to overthrow." (2 Chronicles 25:7-8)

Amaziah should have known this, shouldn't he? You would think he might have remembered how God helped his own grandfather Jehoshaphat win a miraculous victory with a very small army whose weapons were a song and a prayer. But Amaziah forgot. And when he did, God sent someone to remind him that bigger is not necessarily better—or blessed. As it says in Psalm 127:1, "Unless the Lord builds the house, its builders labor in vain." If we attempt to do anything for God without asking Him to be part of it, we are completely wasting our time, and flirting with disaster. Essentially, this is what the man of God told Amaziah. But Amaziah had a tough time swallowing it, especially since he had already paid Israel for the services of their soldiers to the tune of a hundred talents of silver. (That's about 3.4 metric tons of sterling!)

When Amaziah told the prophet about this expenditure, the man simply said, "The Lord can give you much more than that" (2 Chronicles 26:9). This is when Amaziah came to his senses. He dismissed the Israelite troops, who went away more than a little bit ticked off and acted out their rage by raiding villages and towns throughout Judea.

This was a hard way for Amaziah to learn that, with God, obedience is expected—no matter what the cost. When the time came for Judah to fight Edom, God gave Amaziah's army the victory. I'm pretty sure that would not have happened if Amaziah had ignored His warning and retained the Israeli troops.

HOW QUICKLY WE FORGET

Now we reach the point in Amaziah's story where he makes a fatal error. It reminds me of one of those football games where it's down to the last minute of the last quarter. It's been a tough game—touch and go—but the team has rallied under the strategic direction of a great coach. Then, just when they are about to score that turn-around touchdown, one player gets lazy—or maybe a little too cocky. He decides to play the game his own way, rather than following the coach's directions. And, you guessed it, he drops the ball and the other team takes it and runs. Instead of elated cheers, a disappointed moan echoes through the stadium. It's over.

Here's how Amaziah's game played out. After defeating the Edomites, he brought their idols back with him. The account in 2 Chronicles 25:14 says that he "set them up as his own gods, bowed down to them and burned sacrifices to them." (Yes, you read that right.) God was angry. Once again, He sent a prophet to try to talk some sense into Amaziah. The incredulous prophet asked the king,

"Why do you consult this people's gods, which could not save their own people from your hand?" (2 Chronicles 25:15).

This seems like a no-brainer, doesn't it? However, this time Amaziah refused to listen to God's messenger. In fact, he interrupted him with a nasty threat, wielding his power as king. That's when the game was over for Amaziah. It was clear he was not going to listen, so the prophet didn't waste another breath in warning him. He simply said in words to this effect, "You're *so* done Amaziah. No more chances for you."

The next time Amaziah found himself on a battlefield, God withdrew and let him do it his own way. As a result, Judah suffered a terrible defeat and Jerusalem was plundered. Even the temple of God was gutted by the enemy. And chaos reigned in Judah for some time to come.

Although Amaziah did not die in that battle, he never regained God's blessing on this earth. At the end of 2 Chronicles 25 it says, "From the time that Amaziah turned away from following the Lord, they conspired against him in Jerusalem " (vs. 27).

Amaziah spent his last days as a fugitive and was finally murdered. Yet, despite his disappointing decline, God in his great mercy allowed the body of this wayward king to be brought back and buried with his ancestral kings in the city of Judah.

WE FORGET, BUT GOD REMEMBERS

Are you shaking your head in disbelief right about now? After being the beneficiary of God's long-suffering grace and patience, Amaziah's fall seems unbelievable. I don't know about you, but I'm tempted to say, "I would *never* do that." I won't say that, though, because I've learned to never say never.

As a pastor, I've seen many sad instances where believers have walked a long distance with God and received blessing upon blessing only to forget them because they stopped listening to God. Like Amaziah, they did not follow Him wholeheartedly. And a half-hearted faith makes us prone to falter.

Let me close this chapter on a note of hope. In Amaziah's story we also see how, even when we forget God, He remembers us. If reading about Amaziah's mistakes has struck you in a personal way because you identify with them, please don't give up. Amaziah lived in a time when the coming of Jesus was a promise. But we live in a time when that promise has already been fulfilled. We always have the reminder of the cross to assure us that Jesus has taken the responsibility for our spiritual amnesia. We also have the Holy Spirit to cleanse us from the inside out. It is never too late to say, "I forgot, Lord, and I'm sorry." When you do, He'll be right there to reassure you. "You forgot me, but I remember you," He whispers. "Give me your whole heart. All is forgiven, now get off the bench and back into the game."

PLAYING BY THE BOOK
Be committed, not just involved!

Someone said the difference between being involved and committed is like an eggs and ham breakfast. The chicken was involved; the ham was committed! All joking aside, let me ask you a serious question. In your walk with God, are you merely involved (half-hearted) or, have you committed your whole heart to Jesus? Here are some spiritual exercises to test the strength of your "heart muscle."

Worship Workout

Here's a quick test to help you see where you stand. Regarding each of the following habits, circle the letter that describes you best: *I* for involved or *C* for committed. Be honest!

Church Attendance	I	C
Personal ministry	I	C
Bible Study	I	C
Daily devotions	I	C
Prayer time	I	C
Christian fellowship	I	C
Discipleship	I	C
Family worship	I	C
Walking the talk	I	C
Daily Witness	I	C

How many C's did you circle? Hopefully, all of them. If not, ask God to show you which areas are most important to Him and begin working towards a whole-hearted commitment. From time to time, use this list as a "heart check-up" to measure your daily walk.

Trust in the Lord with all your heart and lean not on your own under-standing; in all your ways acknowledge him, and he will make your paths straight. (Proverbs 3:5-6)

FOURTH QUARTER FUMBLES

CHAPTER 6

HEZEKIAH:
Out In Overtime

❧

A game that turned deadly

His name was Donnie Moore, and he was a relief pitcher for the Chicago Cubs, St. Louis Cardinals, Milwaukee Brewers, Atlanta Braves, and California Angels. He was a great ball player, but he made a mistake that he took too much to heart. As a result, his "game" of life turned deadly.

The tragedy began when Donnie Moore, then playing for the Angels, gave up a home run to Boston's Dave Henderson. Not just any home run, though. This home run prevented the Angels from going to the 1986 World Series.

Three years later, that game (along with other contributing factors) triggered a tragedy. Donnie Moore took a gun and fired three shots at his wife. Although none of those bullets hit a fatal mark, the one he put through his own head did. And Donnie Moore's story has become a ghostly warning that games, in sports and in life, can turn deadly. (Hofstetter, "Just a Game?")

READ ALL ABOUT IT:

2 Chronicles 29-32, 2 Kings 18-20 and Isaiah 36-39

In sports and in life, what really matters is not whether you win or lose. It's how you play the game. Even so, what a miserable moment it is when your favorite player on your favorite team has played an outstanding game—only to blow it, just this side of victory. Or, when after years of hard work and diligent effort, your child drops out of school a few weeks before graduation. And how it breaks our hearts to hear about a long-enduring marriage that crumbles because a spouse gave into the temptation to be unfaithful during mid-life.

In God's eyes, playing well means finishing well. It means going the distance with Him. Author Eugene Peterson describes this perfectly in the title of one of his books *A Long Obedience in the Same Direction*. Hezekiah was a king who went a long obedience in the same direction. Yet, as you'll see, he took a late life detour.

When I was doing research for this study of Judah's kings, I was amazed at the amount of information in the Bible about Hezekiah. Yet, unlike David and Solomon, Hezekiah's name is not so well-known to us. You might say Hezekiah is the most famous guy in the Bible that nobody knows much about.

There are 302 verses spanning eleven chapters that tell Hezekiah's illustrious story—four in 2 Chronicles, three in 2 Kings and four more in Isaiah. As we look at his life together I'll touch on the highlights. However, if you take the time to read Hezekiah's whole story, I think you'll agree he lived a rich life—a purpose-filled life, according to God's definition.

Hezekiah was 25 when he became king, and he ruled for 29 years. Remarkably, his righteous reign was sandwiched between those of Ahaz and Manasseh—two of the most *ungodly* kings in the history of Judah. When Hezekiah came to the throne, his country and his people were in a state of spiritual, moral and political decadence. His father Ahaz is considered by many to be the most evil king of Judah's kings. With such a negative legacy, Hezekiah's devotion to God's ways is all the more admirable. After all, what are the odds that the son of a corrupt and evil man will become a god-fearing man of character and integrity? Not great! But Hezekiah beat the odds, and I believe one of the reasons was that his mother, Abijah, embraced a legacy of faith in her birth family that she quietly and diligently passed on to her son. Abijah's family tree included Zechariah, a martyred prophet—and Jehoida, the good priest you may recall from the chapter about Joash. For a Christian mom or dad who is unequally yoked with an unbelieving spouse, here is an encouraging example of how, with God's help, one good parent's nurturing can have a powerful and lasting impact on a child caught in the middle.

This is what happened with Hezekiah. The Bible says that he "did what was right in the eyes of the Lord, just as his father David had done" (2 Chronicles 29:2). Obviously David was *not* Hezekiah's birth father. In fact, about 300 years had passed between the reigns of David and Hezekiah. Yet, the writer of 2 Chronicles links these two men together as father and son because of the *spiritual DNA* they shared.

REVIVAL REAPS RESULTS

When Hezekiah became king, the first thing on his mind was revival, and he didn't waste any time. Traditional worship and the temple of God had been long neglected, and Hezekiah recognized the need for renewal. So, in the very first month of his reign, he ordered that the doors of the Lord's temple be opened and extensive repairs begun. "Now I intend to make a covenant with the Lord, the God of

Israel, so that his fierce anger will turn away from us," he said to the people (2 Chronicles 29:10). Renovations were completed immediately and religious services were reestablished. The Bible says that "Hezekiah and all the people rejoiced at what God had brought about for his people, because it was done so quickly" (2 Chronicles 29:36).

This was just the beginning of a righteous revival in Judah. According to The Merriam-Webster Dictionary, the word revival means "to return or restore to consciousness or life." This is what happened in Judah during Hezekiah's reign. Restoring the temple was like a spark that fanned the dying embers of faith on both a national and personal level. Like the scientific principle of cause and effect, one thing led to another because true revival restores spiritual life — just like the dictionary says. Let's look at five of many positive results that came from Hezekiah's reformation.

#1: WORSHIP

Hezekiah was a true worship leader who inspired his people to repent from their backslidden condition and to return to God with joy and celebration. 2 Chronicles 29 records how Hezekiah assembled the priests and Levites and challenged them to join him in confession that "our fathers were unfaithful . . . they turned their faces away from the Lord's dwelling place and turned their backs on him" (v. 6). Then he urged them to renew their commitment to be effective spiritual leaders. "My sons, do not be negligent now," he said, "for the Lord has chosen you to stand before him and serve him" (v. 11).

#2: UNITY

Inspired by their godly king, the priests and Levites set to work to reestablish worship as the centerpiece of daily life. As the people followed their example, chaos and disorder gave way to unity and harmony. National and personal strength was the natural outgrowth of spiritual reform.

As a pastor and as a parent, I am convicted by this story. It reminds me that, just as God chose Hezekiah, He has chosen *me* to lead my family and my flock. The buck stops here! I am the one appointed to be their worship leader. Every minute of every day, this is my calling. If my faith is joyful, vibrant, and authentic, it will also be contagious. My household and my church will be strong and free from rebellion and discord. We will experience unity. You, too, are chosen by God. What kind of worship leader are you?

#3: ENCOURAGEMENT

In addition to being united, the people were also encouraged. In 2 Chronicles 30:22 and 26 it says that "Hezekiah spoke encouragingly . . . and there was great joy in Jerusalem." Have you ever had the experience of being really disheartened, perhaps even depressed? Once your spirits begin to droop, it can be like falling into a deep dark pit. Down you go. Down, down, down. I don't know about you, but it's hard for me to pull myself up once I start to slip-slide into despair. Yet, isn't it also true that a little encouragement can make a big difference? As a man named George M. Adams (God's Little Devotional Book for Women) once said, "We should seize every opportunity to give encouragement. Encouragement is oxygen to the soul."

Our bodies can't survive without oxygen. Our souls can't thrive without hope. If everyone made an effort to be an encourager, the world would be a happier, healthier, and more hopeful place. With Hezekiah as their encouraging king, Judah was joyful.

#4: GENEROSITY

Another outgrowth of revival in Judah was a surge of generosity. We read about this in 2 Chronicles 31 and learn that Hezekiah again took the lead by contributing "from his own possessions for the morning burnt offerings and for the burnt offerings on the Sabbaths, New Moons and appointed feasts as written in the law of the Lord" (v.

3). Once more, the king asked his people to follow his lead and they obediently responded. In fact, the Bible says that the response was so generous that the tithes of herds, flocks and "holy things dedicated to the Lord" were "piled in heaps" (v. 6). For ministers of finance, this passage is a fantasy dream! In return, God was pleased and verse 8 tells how He "blessed his people."

What a perfect example of the benefits that come when God's people tithe! There is always more than enough to fulfill God's purposes within a church — and to help the needy people He brings to us. I've seen interesting research on this tithing principle. One interesting estimate states that if all Christians in the United States tithed their income, *every* hungry American could be fed in Jesus' name. Equally as important, God would be credited and the Great Commission would be fulfilled in our country. (Just think what would happen if every believer around the world was a tither.)

#5: GOD FIRST

Perhaps the most significant result of Hezekiah's reformation project was the widespread removal of idolatry that had slowly infiltrated the culture of Judaism. Hezekiah's reforms in this area were carried out with intentional determination to get rid of anything that would compete with God for His love and loyalty. In 2 Kings 18:4, we find a description of Hezekiah's war against idolatry:

> He removed the high places, smashed the sacred stones and cut down the Asherah poles. He broke into pieces the bronze snake Moses had made, for up to that time the Israelites had been burning incense to it. (It was called Nehushtan.)

Perhaps you recall the story about Moses and the bronze snake. This goes back to the time when the Israelites were in the wilderness, headed for the Promised Land. They became rebellious, and God sent a plague of poisonous snakes to discipline them. When their leader, Moses, cried out to God for mercy, He gave instructions to make a bronze snake and put it on a pole. Whenever the people looked at the bronze snake in faith, it reminded them of God's mercy and they were healed. For 700 years, the bronze snake had been kept as a sort of museum piece to memorialize what God had done. Somewhere along the line, however, it had ceased to be a symbol and had instead become an idol. The people forgot what the bronze snake stood for—the merciful forgiveness of God, and so this relic became a stumbling block—a false god. Wise King Hezekiah recognized this and destroyed the bronze snake.

You may be puzzled as to why God would have told Moses to make a bronze snake in the first place. To put this in context here, let's just say that God used tangible visual aids like this to instruct the Israelites during the wilderness years. Many biblical scholars maintain that the bronze snake on a pole resembled the cross that lifted Jesus up as a sacrifice for sin in order to defeat Satan. In this sense, the bronze snake foreshadowed the saving sacrifice of Jesus.

As long as we worship what it symbolizes—the sacrifice of Jesus—the cross can be an aid to true worship. However, if we worship the cross rather than Jesus who died on it, we are in danger of making a holy symbol into an idol that can be a stumbling block to true faith.

In a similar way, holidays like Christmas and Easter can cease to be *holy*days when we allow ourselves to be mesmerized by the commercial marketers who exploit these spiritual celebrations. When we do this, our idol becomes the almighty dollar. Anything that jeopardizes our love and loyalty to God can become an idol in our lives. That description includes things we consider to be good—like hobbies, families, friends and, *yes,* (as much as it pains me to admit this) even football.

THE GOING GETS TOUGH

As you can see, Hezekiah's work for the Lord was quite impressive. With so many wonderful things to his credit, we would hope the next line to his story would be "and he lived happily ever after." Sadly, that wasn't the case.

Have you ever noticed that when someone gets really serious about Jesus, their life gets harder instead of easier? It doesn't seem fair, does it? Yet, if we think about this in light of the fact that God has a supernatural enemy, then it makes more sense. Satan doesn't bother much with us until he sees that he's losing his hold on us. Once we begin to see the Light of Christ and follow it, that's when Satan's claws come out and the spiritual warfare begins. That's what happened with Hezekiah, as we see in 2 Chronicles 32. In the first verse it says, "After all that Hezekiah had so faithfully done, Sennacherib king of Assyria came and invaded Judah. He laid siege to the fortified cities, thinking to conquer them for himself."

At this time in history, Assyria was the world's greatest super power. Not only that, the Assyrians were a very cruel and violent people. Their invasion of Judah was a horrible threat and one that could have been met with panic. Instead, Hezekiah trusted God. He called a meeting of his military staff and together they devised a strategic plan to block the water supply to Sennacherib's army. Then Hezekiah assigned military officers over the people—sort of like calling out the National Guard in an emergency. The Bible says that Hezekiah convened an assembly and encouraged his people with these wonderful words:

> Be strong and courageous. Do not be afraid or discouraged because of the king of Assyria and the vast army with him, for there is a greater power with us than with him. With him is only the arm of flesh, but

with us is the Lord our God to help us and to fight our
battles. And the people gained confidence from what
Hezekiah the king of Judah said. (2 Chronicles 32:6-8)

Here is a picture of how we should lead the people in our lives.
Our personal battles may not be against the world's greatest super-
power, but it's a fact of life that we will have battles—and there's a
silver lining we can look for in those combat clouds. You see, when
we trust God and keep our heads about us, He will give us wisdom
and support to deal with whatever comes our way. When I am in
this situation, one of the verses I cling to is 1 Corinthians 10:13. It
says, "God is faithful; he will not let you be tempted beyond what
you can bear. But when you are tempted, he will also provide a way
out so that you can stand up under it." Hezekiah trusted in the faithfulness of God and he looked expectantly for the way out. His own
trust spread through the ranks and strengthened the confidence of
his entire nation. This should also be our goal when we're under
fire—to lift others above their fear by giving them a living example
of trust in God.

THE GOING GETS TOUGHER

When the Assyrians saw that fear wasn't going to work, they
turned to an even more insidious strategy of psychological warfare.
The Assyrian King Sennacherib sent a field commander to tease,
taunt, harass and confuse Hezekiah and his military leaders in an
effort to wear them down. In this biblical story, I am fascinated by the
parallels I see with Satan's methods of chipping away at our faith as
he attempts to twist our thinking and make us question what we know
to be truth. Let me point out a few principles we can draw from 2
Kings 18, the account of the summit meeting between Sennacherib's
field officer and Hezekiah's military commanders.

Satan will try to shake your confidence. The first tactic used was the simple question, "On what are you basing this confidence of yours?" (2 Kings 18:22). By implication, the messenger was questioning the power of God. He knew that a seed of doubt can grow into a choking weed that could kill the trust on which Hezekiah and his people were standing.

Satan will mock you. The second attempt to disarm came in the form of sarcasm and cruel taunting as if to say, "Come now. You are a fool to think you and your God can take us on" (2 Kings 18:23-25).

Satan will lie to you and try to pretend the lie is a message from God. Sennacherib's commander even had the audacity to claim, "The Lord himself told me to march against this country and destroy it" (2 Kings 18:25). This is the kind of satanic lie that has led misguided followers of cults like Heaven's Gate and fanatics like Jim Jones to commit suicide, believing that God was directing them.

Satan will try to terrify and terrorize you. Confused and frightened, the people were more susceptible to the messenger when he urged them, "Do not listen to Hezekiah, for he is misleading you when he says, 'The Lord will deliver us'" (2 Kings 18:33).

Satan will entice you with promises of an "easy way." Once the messenger had undermined the confidence of the people, he could seduce them with false promises. "Make peace and come out to me," he said. "Every one of you will eat from his own vine and fig tree and drink water from his own cistern. Choose life and not death!" (2 Kings 18:31-32) Like a spider spinning a delicate but deadly web, Satan will promise you life. Beware! It's a trap.

Satan will muddle his lies with half-truths to confuse you even more. Finally came the challenging question, "Has any god of any nation ever delivered his land from the hand of the king of Assyria?" (2 Kings 18:33). At this point, Hezekiah's coalition was so confused they couldn't think straight. If they had paused to really consider this, they would have had to reply, "Who cares? *ALMIGHTY GOD* is our God. He can and will deliver us."

AGAINST ALL ODDS

Now comes the part of this story I love to tell. Imagine how those messengers felt as they took all of this tough news back to King Hezekiah in a letter. The enemy had played every card, and the favored team had been chosen. I'm sure Sennacherib's troops were having a party, thinking that victory was a sure thing. They didn't know that Hezekiah had a secret weapon.

When Hezekiah received the letter, he went to the temple and spread it out before the Lord. And then he prayed a simple, sincere prayer—as though he were sitting with God and having a face-to-face conversation. Here is the prayer he prayed:

O Lord, God of Israel, enthroned between the cherubim, you alone are God over all the kingdoms of the earth. You have made heaven and earth. Give ear, O Lord, and hear; open your eyes, O Lord, and see; listen to the words Sennacherib has sent to insult the living God. It is true, O Lord, that the Assyrian kings have laid waste these nations and their lands. They have thrown their gods into the fire and destroyed them, for they were not gods but only wood and stone, fashioned by men's hands. Now, O lord, our God, *deliver us from his hand, so that all kingdoms on earth may know that you alone, O Lord, are God.* (2 Kings 19:14-19)

In this prayer, we see that Hezekiah's motives were pure and righteous. His empire was on the brink of destruction. His life and the lives of thousands under his leadership were in jeopardy. But Hezekiah's only concern was that God's reputation was in question. He asked for deliverance in order to vindicate and glorify his Lord. Nothing more.

The Bible tells us that on that very night the angel of the Lord went out and destroyed 185,000 troops in the Assyrian camp. When the sun rose the next morning, King Sennacherib found carnage in his camp and fled like a dog with his tail between his legs. When the world's mightiest king met Almighty God that day, there was no contest. And yet, this man's heart was not changed by this encounter. Sometime later, Sennacherib was in the temple worshiping "his god Nisroch" when two of his sons murdered him in cold blood.

Are you or someone you care for under attack by the enemy today? Perhaps you've received bad news about your health. Maybe you've lost your job and are facing financial ruin. You may even be fighting to hold your marriage together. Whatever you are facing today, come and spread your concerns on the table before God. Talk to Him with an open and sincere heart. Trust Him like Hezekiah did. If God is first, you'll be a winner no matter what happens.

PRIDE GOES BEFORE THE FALL

What a story—if only it ended here. After such a great and glorious victory for the Lord, it would seem that Hezekiah could retire and take his place in God's Hall of Fame. Not so! Another trial was coming—a personal trial that turned out to be much harder for Hezekiah to handle. Here's what happened:

> Hezekiah became ill and was at the point of death. The prophet Isaiah son of Amoz went to him and said, "This is what the Lord says: Put your house in order, because you are going to die; you will not recover."
>
> Hezekiah turned his face to the wall and prayed to the Lord, "Remember, O Lord, how I have walked before you faithfully and with wholehearted devotion and have done what is good in your eyes." And Hezekiah wept bitterly. (2 Kings 20:1-2)

How would you feel if this happened to you? Hezekiah was only 38 years old—still a relatively young man. As we've just seen, he had lived his life in devoted service to God and led His people faithfully. Then, in the prime of life, he received the news that he was about to die.

Hezekiah did what any of us would do. He did what is the right thing to do. He turned to God, gave Him his pain, wept and prayed. As you might expect, God heard his prayers and answered by instructing Isaiah to order the appropriate medical procedure of the day. Hezekiah responded to the procedure and was healed. God granted fifteen more years of life and also promised another military victory. "I will deliver you and this city," said the Lord, "for my sake and the sake of my servant David" (2 Kings 20:6).

This seems like a happy ending, doesn't it? Unfortunately, though, Hezekiah made some mistakes during those extra fifteen years of life—mistakes that go down in history as failures. This was Hezekiah's fourth quarter fumble. In the end, it was not a vast army that brought this king down. It was a proud heart. It came after a lifetime of success and accomplishments and after his faith had endured the supreme test we've just looked at.

The play came down this way. Hezekiah received letters and a gift from a man named Merodach-Baladan. He was the son of the King of Babylon. In light of what we know about Babylon now, we might think that this was someone very important and powerful. However, at that time, Babylon was only a little backwoods country. The letters and gifts were delivered by messengers and Hezekiah decided to show off a bit for his visitors. The Bible says he "showed them all that was in his storehouses—the silver, the gold, the spices, and the fine oil—his armory and everything found among his treasures. There was nothing in his palace or in all his kingdom that Hezekiah did not show them" (2 Kings 20:12-13). This was not a wise move. It might be compared to the president of the United States revealing America's top secrets to a little country like Togo! What displeased God most was Hezekiah's arrogant and reckless attitude. Isaiah the prophet was sent to confront Hezekiah with this solemn proclamation:

> Hear the word of the Lord: The time will surely come when everything in your palace, and all that your fathers have stored up until this day, will be carried off to Babylon. Nothing will be left, says the Lord. And some of your descendants, your own flesh and blood, that will be born to you, will be taken away. (2 Kings 20:16-18)

Hezekiah was immediately convicted of his sin and repented. But this time, God did not issue a pardon. Isaiah's prophecy was fulfilled 150 years later when the people of Judah, including Hezekiah's own relatives, were dragged off in exile to Babylon.

OUT IN OVERTIME

I don't know about you, but this sad twist to such a glorious story leaves me stunned. Many students of the Bible feel like it might have been better if Hezekiah had submitted when God said "time's up" rather than pleading for "time out" and negotiating the extra 15 years of life. In light of what happened during those years, it could be said that Hezekiah fumbled in overtime. I'll leave it up to you to decide on that issue.

Here's something to think about as you ponder Hezekiah's story. Facing death is a very different prospect for Christians than it is for unbelievers. If you have no eternal hope, death is the worst thing that can happen to you, but for the redeemed in Christ, there is something far worse than death. Failing God and bringing disgrace on His name is the most devastating thing of all.

There's an interesting verse in Isaiah 57:1 that says, "The righteous perish and no one ponders it in his heart; devout men are taken away . . . to be spared from evil." Perhaps this can help us when a life is cut short earlier than our expectations and we are prone to ask why. I certainly wrestled with questions when my sister passed away at the age of 54. Whenever an innocent baby or a very young child dies before ever having the chance to really live, it's tough not to shake a fist at God and ask, "Why, Lord . . . why?" In puzzling times like these, it's helpful to remember that God knows the future, and that sometimes death is an act of His loving and merciful protection. It's easier to release someone you love at *any* age if you have the eternal perspective that God knows what is best. No matter when that time comes, we can take comfort from another verse from Isaiah 57: "Those who walk uprightly enter into peace; they find rest as they lie in death" (vs. 2).

Please don't misunderstand what I'm saying. It's one thing to preach about this. It's another to live by it. Like everyone else, I want to be on this planet for a long time. So when my wife Kimberly makes my sandwiches with that gross non-fat mayonnaise and piles my plate high with salad instead of a juicy steak, I eat every bite dutifully. I exercise and get my annual physical. I'm doing everything I can to live as long as I can. But death, from the eternal perspective, is not what I fear most. I can tell you with all honesty that I would rather die at age 50, living faithfully for Jesus, than to mess up spiritually while pushing 80. When you look at Hezekiah's life and the mistakes he made in the additional years after his illness, you can really say that it might have been wiser and better for him to submit to God's perfect way.

PLAYING BY THE BOOK

Revival for Survival!

Hezekiah's reign started with spiritual revival and was sustained by the power of prayer. But 25 years later, he lost his zeal and fell into the sin of pride. Constant prayer plus regular doses of revival can help us avoid being "out in overtime." Here are a few ideas to get you started on your revival regimen.

Worship Workout

Spiritual habits, like health habits, are only effective when they are faithfully practiced. By now, I hope you have scheduled a daily appointment to talk with God earnestly about the things that concern you. As prayer becomes more and more a part of your life, you may find it helpful to keep a prayer journal—noting your prayer concerns and dating them for reference. If journaling seems too overwhelming, make a Hezekiah file. Jot short prayer notes on small pieces of paper and put them in a file folder or manila envelope. You can also use this file to hold copies of important documents like medical reports, unexpected bills, your church's newsletter, etc. When you pray, spread your file out before the Lord and give the contents to God as Hezekiah did when he received Sennacherib's threats.

Offensive Weapon: Strengthen your team!

Building God's *team* is part of our responsibility as Christian parents, children, friends, and neighbors. There are many ways that you can help spread "revival" through the ranks. Meeting together to pray and study God's Word, sending notes of encouragement, holding one another accountable to live God's way are just a few examples of how you can strengthen the teammates God has put into your life.

The law of the Lord is perfect, reviving the soul. (Psalm 19:7)

FOURTH QUARTER FUMBLES

CHAPTER 7

JOSIAH:
Playing For Keeps

Famous Fumbles

Milli Vannilli

Communism in Russia

Elizabeth Taylor and Richard Burton

The Berlin Wall

Michael Jackson and Lisa Marie Presley

Richard Nixon's Presidency

Elizabeth Taylor and John Warner

Edsel

Enron Stock

Whitney Houston

Jimmy Swaggart

Elizabeth Taylor and Larry Fortensky

The Titanic

Elvis Presley

ValueJet Airlines

Glenn Gunderson's hair

What do these have in common?

Good start . . . bad finish!

READ ALL ABOUT IT:

2 Chronicles 34-35.

A fter an evangelistic meeting, the famous preacher D.L. Moody was asked how many people were saved that night.

"Two and a half," he replied decisively.

"You must mean two adults and one child?" came the counter question.

"No, I mean one adult and two children," Moody replied. "Because the adult just has half his life to follow God. But the two children have their entire life to live for God." (Child Evangelism Fellowship Singapore)

What a wonderful blessing it is to follow God from an early age! One of the first things we learn about a king named Josiah is that "when he was still young, he began to seek the God of his father David" (2 Chronicles 34:3).

When Josiah began his serious search for God, he was only about 16 years old and he had already been king of Judah for half of his life—since he was just eight years old. (Be careful not to confuse this boy king with Joash—Josiah's ancestor who ruled much earlier in Judah's history. Like that ancestor, Josiah had the heavy responsibility of leadership thrust upon him very early in life.) You'll see as you read through this chapter that when Josiah made that early decision to follow God, it was a heartfelt commitment. With childlike faith, he made a choice to play for keeps on God's team. The

Bible confirms that Josiah continued to do "what was right in the eyes of the Lord . . . not turning aside to the right or to the left" (2 Chronicles 34:2).

Josiah reigned a good long time—for 31 years. Then, at the age of 39, he died. To us, 39 is young. If someone dies at that age today, we consider it to be a life tragically cut short. We are perplexed over the wasted potential. The lost years seem such a shame, especially when the deceased person has lived an exemplary and productive life, as Josiah did. A death that seems premature sometimes causes us to question God's decision. It raises questions in our minds like, "Does God really care about us in a personal way?" Or, "Does God truly have a plan?" And even, "Is God really in control?"

You may wrestle with questions like this as you learn more about Josiah. As you do, keep in mind the story of Hezekiah that we examined in Chapter 6. As you recall, God gave Hezekiah the extra time he asked for. However, during that time, Hezekiah made some very tragic mistakes that cause us to question whether those additional years were really a good thing.

In Josiah's case, just the opposite happened. There were no extra years. He died at 39. But, as you'll see, his life counted for God until the very end. This reminds me of a lighthearted story about an elderly couple who died and went to Heaven. As they toured around together, they were awed and amazed at the wonders of their new eternal home. Delighted by what they saw, the husband turned to his wife and said, "If you hadn't made me eat all those bran muffins, we could have been here a lot sooner!"

Of course, this is a joke. But it makes a point worth pondering. Death can be seen as a sad thing—or a glad thing—depending on your perspective. If we trust in God's perfect timing, we can have confidence that even a premature death is part of His plan. If we really believe that, if we really trust Him, if we've really surrendered our destiny to Him, we don't need to question His decisions. Whether He gives us a long life or a short one, every day is entrusted to us with the responsibility to live each minute for Him. Josiah was intent on doing this, from a very early age.

AGAINST ALL ODDS

That Josiah turned decisively to the Lord when he was so young was quite remarkable. In fact, I would say it was a miracle. You see, Josiah ascended to the throne when spiritual and moral corruption was at an all-time high in Judah.

To give you a contemporary frame of reference, imagine if an 8-year-old boy became the leader of Iraq today. As that boy went through early childhood and interacted with his dad and other people who were immersed in that culture, what would be the likelihood that he would even know about God, much less seek Him? The odds would be unfavorable, wouldn't you say? Just as the odds were against Josiah choosing well-grounded faith in God as the foundation for his political, social, and cultural platform.

Idolatry was widespread. The temple was in ruins. The faith of Judah's people had been watered down by outside influences. Parents were not teaching their children God's Word. Everybody was doing their own thing. You might say that people practiced "pick 'n save" religion—accepting what they liked and tossing out anything that made them uncomfortable. Plus, their king was only eight years old!

Sounds like a setup for disaster. Once again we see how God will intervene in humanly impossible situations. He takes the responsibility to preserve His holy ways and righteous truths. He does this for His glory and the good of the people He loves. I can't pretend to know why God chose Josiah, but I can make an educated guess that perhaps it was because he knew Josiah had a heart that would respond. And so God positioned a man named Hilkiah, who was high priest at the time, to help and guide the young king. Hilkiah likely assumed the role of teacher, counselor, and spiritual mentor to the boy ruler—teaching Josiah to love the Lord, and modeling what he taught. With this holy influence, Josiah grew strong in mind, body, and spirit and beat the odds.

BURIED TREASURE

Around the age of 20, Josiah was ready to tackle the huge job God had entrusted to him. He launched a widespread cleanup campaign in Judah that included purging the land of idolatry, repairing the temple of God, and ultimately led to the last great revival before the Babylonian exile.

Things began to roll during the process of purifying the temple, when a buried treasure was discovered. Here's how the story goes:

> Hilkiah the priest found the book of the Law of the Lord that had been given through Moses. Then Shaphan the secretary informed the king, "Hilkiah the priest has given me a book." And Shaphan read from it in the presence of the king. When the king heard the words of the Law, he tore his robes. He gave these orders . . . "Go and inquire of the Lord for me and for the remnant in Israel and Judah about what is written in this book that has been found. Great is the Lord's anger that is poured out on us because our fathers have not kept the word of the Lord; they have not acted in accordance with all that is written in this book." (2 Chronicles 34:14, 18-21)

There are several things that stand out in these five verses. First, it seems tragic that God's Word had been neglected to the point that it had fallen beneath the rubble. Even the remnant of godly priests did not seem to know that this book was God's Holy Word when they uncovered it as they were cleaning up the temple. Still, they instinctively knew that it was an important book and brought it right to the king.

On a mission trip to the Philippines, our junior high pastor was deeply impressed to see how the people there were ecstatic to receive a copy of the Bible. In America, we still have the precious freedom to be able to purchase a Bible in just about any bookstore. We can hold Bible studies in our homes and read God's Word openly from the pulpits of our churches. Sure, we may be teased or harassed from time to time. We may even be excluded from some social circles because of our alliance with Christ. However, we're still free to follow Him—and to own, read, and practice God's Word. I'm afraid this is a blessing we take for granted. In many, many places throughout the world, it is a rare thing for people to have a personal copy of the Bible. In some areas, it is quite dangerous to read and practice God's Word. In some, people are even imprisoned, tortured or martyred if they are caught with a Bible in their possession. It seems hard to believe, but it's true.

Your Bible is perhaps the most valuable treasure you own. Has it fallen into the rubble of a life that is cluttered with busyness? If so, I urge you to find it, dust it off, and begin to discover the powerful blessings God has for you in His book. That's what Josiah did, and this brings me to the second lesson that stands out in this story.

As we read about the discovery of God's Word in the temple, it's impressive to see the impact it had when Josiah heard it for the first time. At first, it actually precipitated a crisis, because it was immediately clear to Josiah that his nation and people were living on borrowed time. The words he heard included stern warnings about consequences for behaviors that are offensive to God, and Josiah knew that his people had been doing many of these things for years.

115

When they heard the warnings, terror struck their hearts—and rightfully so. At once, they got it. God's judgment was past due.

Fortunately, Josiah was leading the way, and he paid attention. He didn't hem and haw and go away and think it over. He didn't consult with human advisors. Because Josiah's heart was right with God, he instinctively knew that their only hope was to repent and turn back from their sins. He responded immediately, tearing his robes and crying out to God. As king, he took the lead and repented with a heart that was broken. And people began to fall in line. Religious rituals, like Passover, were reinstated. Once again, under Josiah's leadership, God's ways became the ways of His people. This was the beginning of revival in Judah.

LET'S GET SERIOUS!

True revival always starts with a serious consideration of God's Word. When people read God's Word, take it to heart and apply it to their lives, the result is transformation. You see, the Bible is not just an exciting, interesting book you read to relax. It is all that and more, because the words in the Bible were written by God himself through the inspiration of His Holy Spirit. These are supernatural words that are eternally relevant. When people recognize this, it's a trademark of revival, and true revival should not be limited to events like Billy Graham crusades or Women of Faith conferences. These events are wonderful ways to keep our faith vibrant and to expose others to Christ. Revival, however, should not be something we experience once or twice a year at a gathering. Revival should be a way of life.

Is revival a way of life for you and your family? If not, I challenge you to make a commitment to pray for revival every day. Pray for the people in your life who have fallen away. Pray for our world that is slipping deeper and deeper into spiritual confusion and darkness. Pray for yourself, that God will guard you against falling into the subtle sin of complacency.

The 21st century is not so different from the time of Josiah. It's easy to become discouraged and heavy-hearted over the apostasy we see all around us. It's important that we not take it lightly. But we don't need to give up. It's not hopeless. And we can be encouraged by a look at our history.

Because of our founding principles, many people assume that, in the beginning, America was red hot for God and just gradually cooled off over the years. This is not true. In fact, the darkest time for faith in American history was probably in the early part of the 18th century. In those days, on-fire Christians were few and far between. Then, in the mid-1700's, right before the Revolutionary War, there was a dynamic young preacher from Massachusetts named Jonathan Edwards. Like Josiah, he read God's Word with a responsive heart. Through Edwards, God ignited a spark of faith that blazed into a revival that swept across our country. This revival came to be known as the Great Awakening.

At that time, there were only one or two Christians at Harvard— even though this prestigious university was founded as a Christian school. It was the same situation at Yale. Despite their Christian roots, these universities had been overtaken by secular intellectualism. Christian students had to meet in secret to pray, study the Bible, and have fellowship with other believers. That's how bad things were just prior to the war that made America "one nation under God."

When the Great Awakening happened, there was a tremendous turning back to God. People got serious about God's Word, just like Josiah did. The timing of this historic revival couldn't have been better, and we can see how God was at work. It turned people back to God, just before the founding of independence for this great nation. That's why there was so much Christian influence at the beginning of our nation's history. This influence still touches us today. We see it in the Declaration of Independence, the Constitution and all of the formal documents that established our national identity. Our founding fathers were dedicated people. They were serious about the things of God—as a result of a revival that began with one man. A man like Josiah.

Because of Josiah's spiritual leadership and wide-sweeping reforms, God postponed judgment. Eventually it would come—and it did, in 586 B.C. when Judah was dragged into exile in Babylon. But we can see from Josiah's story that God is merciful and we should not lose hope.

AN ERROR IN JUDGEMENT

A few years ago, Rick Warren wrote a book that started a revival in our churches. I'm sure you remember that book. It was on the best seller list for months and it was called *The Purpose Driven Life*. I think this title describes Josiah's life but even though Josiah's life was purposeful, it wasn't perfect. There was a time when he made a serious error in judgment. It's important that we look carefully at his fourth quarter fumble, because it's the kind of thing that can so easily trip us up as Christians. Josiah made an erroneous judgment call, based on what he thought was right and good and pleasing to God. Let's look together at what happened:

> After all this, when Josiah had set the temple in order, Neco king of Egypt went up to fight at Carchemish on the Euphrates, and Josiah marched out to meet him in battle. But Neco sent messengers to him saying, "What quarrel is there between you and me, O king of Judah? It is not you I am attacking at this time, but the house with which I am at war. God has told me to hurry, so stop opposing God, who is with me, or he will destroy you."

> Josiah, however, would not turn away from him, but disguised himself to engage him in battle. He would not listen to what Neco had said at God's command but went to fight him on the plain of Megiddo.
>
> Archers shot King Josiah, and he told his officers, "Take me away; I am badly wounded." So they took him out of his chariot, put him on the other chariot he had and brought him to Jerusalem, where he died. (2 Chronicles 35:20-36:1)

This ending to Josiah's wonderful story brings up a red flag for us as believers. Sometimes in our effort to follow God, we back ourselves into a narrow place that is bound by restrictions we believe are ordained by God. We forget that God himself is not defined by the boundaries we place around ourselves.

I need to be very careful how I present this point to you. I do not want you to misunderstand. I am not saying that we can toss all care to the wind and say, "If God is with me, anything goes. I can live in the world and do whatever they do." This contradicts everything I said earlier about getting serious about God's Word.

What I am saying is that we have to be careful about assuming that God cannot—or will not—use someone else to guide, teach and help us, just because that person is not a Christian. Josiah made a fatal error when he refused to listen to good counsel from an unbeliever. On this occasion, he closed his mind without seeking God's enlightenment. He made an assumption that God could not, or would not, speak to him through the pagan king of Egypt. It was an incorrect assumption, it placed limits on God, and it may have even been a missed opportunity to witness to King Neco. Like Josiah, we often make similar assumptions and, when we do, we're in danger because our attitude is presumptuous. I realize there is a fine line to walk—between our devotion to what we *know* about God and His expectations and our willing commitment to trust Him when His ways are outside the scope of our human understanding. The key point is to remember this story when you are faced with a tough judgment call, and to take the time to pray and listen for God to confirm your decision.

HAPPILY EVER AFTER

There is good news I can share at the end of this chapter. Although Josiah's life wasn't perfect, it was very close. There is not a question in my mind about whether Josiah is in Heaven today. Our brother in faith who has gone before us is no doubt living happily ever after. By looking at his life and using it as a model for our own, we have a better chance of crossing the finish line without fumbling along the way.

The prophet Jeremiah eulogized Josiah with these wonderful words—words we would be wise to live by: "He did what was right and just, so all went well with him" (Jeremiah 22:15b).

PLAYING BY THE BOOK
Hidden Treasure

Josiah's revival began when he discovered God's Word buried in the rubble of the temple. He didn't place it on a bookshelf or in a display case. He opened and read it and challenged others to follow his lead. Your Bible is a treasure! How serious are you about the Word of God?

Worship Workout

When Josiah found God's Word, he immediately shared it. Who in your life needs to discover the treasure of God's Word—your spouse, your child, a friend? Here's an upbeat, non-threatening way to share your favorite verses with someone who needs to know God in a more personal way. Purchase a small box, one that your friend or loved one would want to keep on their dresser or bedside table. Fill it with little scrolls of paper, each one with a hand-written promise from God's Word. A few suggestions are printed below to get you started making a Blessing Box for someone you care about. You'll also be blessed yourself as you search through your Bible for more promises to include in your gift.

John 3:16: Promise of salvation
Jeremiah 29:11: Hope for the future
Romans 8:28: Good can come from evil
Lamentations 3:22-23: God's faithfulness
Joshua 1:9: God is with you
1 John 1:9: God forgives

Do not merely listen to the word . . . Do what it says. (James 1:22)

FOURTH QUARTER FUMBLES

CHAPTER 8

UZZIAH:
The Marathoner

THE MAN WHO FINISHED LAST

The 1986 New York City Marathon was a race to remember. With 20,000 runners positioned at the starting line, the competition was fierce. Who would be first to finish, and how quickly would that moment come? Just 2 hours, 11 minutes and 6 seconds later, an Italian athlete named Deanni Poli crossed the finish line and won the race. As impressive as Mr. Poli's race might be, it wasn't the most memorable effort. What made the 1986 New York City Marathon unforgettable was not the man who finished first, but the man who finished last.

His name was Bob Wieland. It took him 4 days, 2 hours, 47 minutes and 17 seconds to complete the course—making it the slowest race in the history of the New York City Marathon. Why did it take Mr. Wieland so long? Because 17 years earlier his legs were blown off while he was serving America in Vietnam. He ran with his arms, pulling himself along—one arm's length at a time. It would have been easier to drop out. Or simply to sit and watch. But Bob Wyland was a marathoner at heart. He started the race and he didn't stop until he crossed the finish line—last, but certainly not least. (Bud Wieland, Wikepedia)

READ ALL ABOUT IT:

2 Chronicles 26.

I have a confession to make. You may find this hard to believe, but football is not *really* my game. Even though the inspiration for this book began with my love of football, God didn't design me to be a quarterback. He wired me to be a runner.

Back in high school and later in college, I was on the track team. Now, there's a sport with a variety of slots to fill! Running, speed walking, jumping, vaulting—there are many competitive events for the athlete who excels in track. As my coaches worked with me, it became evident that my God-given talent was to be a *marathoner* rather than a *sprinter*.

What's the difference? I can tell you in a word: distance. A marathoner is a long-distance runner whose focus is on sustained success, whereas a sprinter has a shorter race to run. Speed, from start to finish, is essential for the sprinter. However, for the marathoner whose race course is much longer, it's more important to establish a sustainable pace.

The old saying that "slow and steady wins the race" describes what I call a marathoner mindset and, concerning spiritual matters, this is the mindset to have. When we decide to run with God, our focus must be on a life-long sustained relationship with Him. We want to get on His track, build spiritual stamina, and pace ourselves to go the distance—all the way to Heaven. To finish God's race, our progress needs to be sure and steady, and we need to always keep our eyes on the finish line. This is the kind of mindset King Uzziah had. As I look at his track record, he reminds me of a marathoner.

A LEGACY OF LONGEVITY

Uzziah is also known by the name Azariah, and you'll see him called by both names in the Bible. The name Uzziah was his throne name, whereas his personal name was Azariah. To avoid confusion, I'll refer to him as Uzziah throughout this chapter.

Uzziah was a 16-year-old teenager when he became king. His father was Amaziah, and you may recall him as the king who was half-hearted about God. Apparently his parenting heart was firmly grounded, though, because his son brought to the throne a determined focus on faith that he probably learned from his dad.

You might say Uzziah had marathoner DNA. This is one of the qualities I love most about my church family. In fact, a key reason I was drawn to our church was its impressive legacy of longevity. Throughout its more than 146 years of history, lead pastors of our church have served an average of fifteen to twenty years and other staff members have a similar impressive record. If you look at our membership records, you can see that our congregation has also remained steady and committed over the years. Our members don't come and go. They are lifers. That's what I mean by marathoner DNA, and it's a sign of a healthy church.

I think Uzziah would have fit in very well at Purpose Church. His reign was long and healthy. The Bible says that "he reigned in Jerusalem fifty-two years" and that "he did what was right in the eyes of the Lord" (2 Chronicles 26:3-4). He was a marathoner king who respected God and recognized that His Word held the guidelines for living a godly life.

Like many of the other kings we've studied, Uzziah had a spiritual mentor. His name was Zechariah (not the Old Testament prophet, Zechariah). This Zechariah was probably the spiritual coach who was most responsible for instructing Uzziah in the fear of God—the trainer who held this king accountable to stay in shape spiritually.

In 2 Chronicles 26:5 it says that "As long as (Uzziah) sought the Lord, God gave him success." This simple statement holds the key to being a spiritual marathoner. If we apply it to our lives, we can be successful workers for God while we are here on earth—and build a legacy of faithful longevity for our children and others who follow in our footsteps. Another scripture that elaborates this biblical principle says:

> Trust in the Lord with all your heart and lean not on your own understanding; in **all** your ways acknowledge him, and he will make your paths straight. (Proverbs 3:5-6)

This is a great verse to cling to when life's race seems endless, because it reminds us that God takes on the responsibility to get us through. All He asks from us is our total, committed trust. A few years ago, I took a little time to get away and seek God's guidance for our church's pastoral and administrative staff. I focused my prayer time on asking the Lord, "What can we do to have more of a spiritual dependence on You?" Being able to hear His answer required this kind of focused trust.

In our ministry, Tuesday is the day that kicks off our week. Sunday is like the finish line—with four worship services and Sunday school for all age groups. Monday is our day of rest. For years, our staff has come together every Tuesday morning for a time of corporate worship and prayer. This is a good practice, aimed at acknowledging God's lordship and trusting Him to direct our path as we move forward into each week of ministry. However, as I continued to seek God, He strongly impressed me that we need to worship and pray together *daily*.

Of course, this makes sense. Still, I had concerns. God has blessed our church with growth and He has also called us to many outreach ministries. We have a lot of work to do every single day, and it takes more hours to do it than there are in any given day. I took these concerns to God. "Lord, we are already stretched thin for work time," I prayed. "If we spend time every morning in worship and prayer, how will we have enough time to get our work done?"

Again I was strongly impressed. I knew without a doubt that I had not misunderstood. I felt God was saying, "Glenn, just lead your staff in obedience and I will expand your time." He didn't tell me how He would do this. He just asked me, as lead pastor, to trust Him. Has God ever asked you to do something that you knew with your mind you were incapable of doing? This was the way I felt, but I went back to my staff and, together, we obeyed this direction from the Lord. Now we pray and worship with a spirit of dependency *every* morning and a remarkable thing has happened. Our work has been propelled by the spiritual wind of God ever since we stepped out in obedient faith to make Him first in all that we do. God is working through the ministries of our church in even mightier ways than He has in the past. I wholeheartedly believe it is because of our response to His call to trust and obey.

Over the course of Uzziah's lifetime, as long as he practiced this same principle, he was fruitful. What about you? As a believer, do you have marathoner DNA? Will you leave behind a legacy of spiritual longevity? It's never too late to get on track with God and start running His race.

AN IMPRESSIVE TRACK RECORD

Uzziah got on track early and, for most of his 52-year-long reign, he appears to have kept his eyes on God and followed His course faithfully. In 2 Chronicles 26, there is a detailed summary of his accomplishments and contributions as Judah's king, including:

- God gave Uzziah victory in battles against the Philistines, Arabs, and Meunites: 2 Chr 26:6-7.

- The Lord blessed Uzziah with success in breaking down walls and rebuilding ruins in the aftermath of war: 2 Chr 26:7.

- The city of Jerusalem was built up, fortified and protected by towers under Uzziah's direction: 2 Chr 26:9.

- Judah's infrastructure was well-established under Uzziah's leadership. Cisterns were dug in the desert and herds of livestock grazed the foothills and plains: 2 Chr 26:10.

- The entire nation prospered. Families had work to do that enabled them to live well—in the fields, vineyards, hills, and fertile lands around Jerusalem: 2 Chr 26:10.

- Uzziah put a well-trained and equipped military system in place, with over 307,000 trained soldiers, 2,600 officers, sophisticated weaponry and skillful strategic advisors. No wonder Judah's enemies kept their distance: 2 Chr 26:11-14.

- A capable staff of royal officials helped Uzziah manage the affairs of state wisely and efficiently: 2 Chr 26:11.

- Uzziah's fame "spread far and wide" because God's blessing was upon him: 2 Chr 26:8, 15.

These were golden years in Judah. If only they had lasted forever! But, as Uzziah grew more and more successful, he fell into a trap that has caused many a man (and woman) to stumble. Unfortunately, power often corrupts. And, Uzziah's growing power ultimately undermined his spiritual strength and caused his downfall.

POWER CORRUPTS

I've heard that for every ten people who can handle failure, only one can handle success. I don't really know how true this is if you're weighing success on secular scales but from a Christian perspective, I would definitely agree—and might even venture to say that the odds of success are even less likely than one in ten.

I don't know about you but during tough times, I tend to draw closer to God. When something comes up that completely overwhelms me, there's no question in my mind that I can't face it alone. I run to God in prayer. I search His Word for guidance and strength and cling to the wisdom He never fails to show me in my open Bible. Worship and fellowship with my Christian friends and family members is never sweeter or more sustaining than when the chips are down. I couldn't get by without them.

I'm sorry to say that good times can have exactly the opposite impact on my walk with the Lord. When things go well, I tend to feel pretty self-confident. It's not that I reject God. I simply am not as aware of my desperate need for Him. A subtle seed of arrogance can take root during these times and, before I know it, I'm off doing my own thing. Then what happens? Because I'm God's child, He's not going to let me wander too far down this path. So along comes a trial to kick the wind out of my sails and to humble me back into an awareness of my total human helplessness and my need to let God take over. This can be a vicious cycle, and pride is perhaps the most common trigger.

MAN ON A MOONWALK

At the height of his power and success as a king, Uzziah stumbled over this flaw in human nature. Like 90% of us, he couldn't handle success. What a shame, after such an illustrious track record. We want to shake our head in exasperation and say, "How could this happen?" Believe me, it can happen. And it does—even to people who are spiritual marathoners like Uzziah. So how can we avoid the stumbling block of pride? I'm going to answer that question by telling you about a man who went walking on the moon.

Depending on your age, you may or may not have been around in 1969 when two American astronauts became the first human beings in world history to land a spacecraft on the moon. What a great day! People the world over huddled together around television sets to watch this awesome event, the culmination of years of scientific effort and courageous risk-taking. As astronauts Buzz Aldrin and Neil Armstrong took their first feather-light steps on the moon, the whole earth cheered.

If ever two men could say, "Look at us, we're amazing," these two could. This was a huge accomplishment that inherently brought with it the temptation for humans to take the credit, but one of those astronauts was a Christian. Long before he took that first moonwalk, a red flag went up in Buzz Aldrin's mind. To ensure that God got the credit, he developed a plan of action based on something Jesus said when He was training His disciples. He wasn't sending them off to the moon, but the walk they were getting ready for would be viewed through the portals of Heaven—every step cheered and applauded by God himself and an audience of angels. This was no less a historic mission than walking on the moon and, as they prepared for it, Jesus warned them not to try to do it alone. He said, "apart from me you can do nothing" (John 15:5).

Buzz Aldrin took this statement to heart as he prepared for his moonwalk. He made a plan so that when he stepped out of the spacecraft and the spotlight was on him, he'd remember to praise and worship God. With millions of human ears listening intently, Aldrin recited John 15:5, reminding the world that this amazing accomplishment was only possible through God's leading. Then he took communion on the moon. Through this example, one small step for mankind became a glorious leap for the Lord.

There is a point to this story, and the point is to have a plan. From here to the moon, wherever life takes us, pride is an ever-present danger. If we are not prepared, it will cause us to stumble and prevent us from a victorious (and glorious) finish. That's what happened to Uzziah.

OUT OF HIS LEAGUE

Uzziah's downfall began with a subtle change in his character that led him to fail a critical test and finally ended with a tragic consequence. The root cause of this downhill slide was pride. Throughout the Bible there are numerous warnings about the dangers of pride, including:

"When pride comes, then comes disgrace . . ."
(Proverbs 11:2)

"Pride goes before destruction, a haughty spirit before a fall."
(Proverbs 16:18)

"God opposes the proud but gives grace to the humble."
(1 Peter 5:5b)

In 2 Chronicles 26:16 it says that "after Uzziah became powerful, his pride led to his downfall." Because of all that we have learned about Uzziah's youth and most of his reign, I believe this sin of pride was like an insidious condition, such as Alzheimer's disease, that invades the body, slowly undermines strength and gradually steals away health. At first the symptoms are subtle. In time, they become so pronounced that they strip away the very essence of personhood. Over time, Uzziah's mindset gradually became self-focused rather than God-focused until finally this self-centeredness became so extreme that he was no longer satisfied to merely be king of Judah. Instead, Uzziah wanted to be a *priest*-king.

At first, this may appear to be spiritual and noble. After all, wouldn't his desire to be priest-king indicate that Uzziah merely wanted to be more righteous and holy? However, God has reserved the right to be Priest-King for only one person—His son, Jesus Christ. In trying to take this role, Uzziah was attempting to enter into God's presence in his own way—not according to God's way. This focus on "my way" is a trademark of the New Age movement that is leading so many people astray today. There is a consensus of opinion that "Anything goes. I can do anything I please." But in John 14:6, God says that Jesus is "*the* way," not *a* way. God, as Creator of mankind, is the only Person who has the right to make the rules.

Another position taken by followers of the New Age movement maintains, "God can't tell me how I can approach Him. I don't have to follow Jesus to get there, I can take my own path." This attitude brings to mind a big buffet of all kinds of food where people can walk through and take a little of this, a little of that. Some people today believe they can take a dab of Jesus, a dollop of Buddha, and maybe a tidbit of Scientology. God says, "No. You must come the way I direct you, and there is *no* compromise." By His very nature, God alone has the right to decide how we come to Him. When we try to do it our way, we are attempting to usurp His sovereignty. That's pride, and it has caused many a soul to stumble and fall—including our royal marathoner, Uzziah.

Unfortunately, he became so intent upon being a priest-king that he actually entered the temple with the intent to perform a priestly duty. At this point, the priests that God had appointed took courage and confronted their king, saying "It is not right for you, Uzziah, to burn incense to the Lord. That is for the priests, the descendants of Aaron . . . Leave the sanctuary, for you have been unfaithful; and you will not be honored by the Lord God" (2 Chronicles 26:18).

131

If only Uzziah had heeded this warning, perhaps he would have come to his senses and recovered his spiritual stride. Instead, Uzziah became angry and lashed out at the priests. Immediately, right there in the temple, God struck him with leprosy. It began with an outbreak on his forehead, and Uzziah knew at once that his days of power and glory were over. The biblical account goes on to say that "King Uzziah had leprosy until the day he died. He lived in a separate house—leprous, and excluded from the temple of the Lord. Jotham his son had charge of the palace and governed the people of the land" (2 Chronicles 26:21).

POST-SEASON VICTORY

I realize that to some, God's judgement of Uzziah may seem overly harsh. If you are one of those people, let me encourage you not to shut your mind—or your Bible—just yet. Turn to 2 Chronicles 27, and you'll read about Uzziah's son, Jotham. If you do this, perhaps you'll feel like there's a happy ending to this story after all. Jotham's wonderful life makes me want to edit that familiar saying: "Like father like son, only better!"

When ranked with Judah's good kings, Jotham takes the gold. He is the only one without even a slight fourth quarter fumble—a godly man any Christian dad would be proud of. A man who made his human father proud—and brought glory and honor to God, from start to finish. A true spiritual marathoner.

No doubt Jotham learned much from his father Uzziah. The tragic fall from God's grace that Uzziah suffered towards the end may have even helped Jotham to avoid falling into the same fatal trap of pride.

Jotham is a human example of how our children can be our happy ending. God's child Jesus takes that principle to its ultimate fulfillment. When we've run off-course (no matter how far or how late), Jesus can get us back on track and give us a happy ending in life. Remember the key? In the words of an old beloved hymn:

Trust and obey, for there's no other way

To be happy in Jesus, but to trust and obey.

PLAYING BY THE BOOK
Building a Marathon Mindset

To go the distance with God, you need to have a marathoner's mindset. In your worship workout this week, focus on developing a plan to fill your days with praise. Pray against pride and make a commitment to trust and obey God as you face each day's challenges.

Worship Workout

Here are two ideas to help you and your family practice praising God on a daily basis:

Personal Plan: In addition to your prayer and study time, cultivate a habit of praising God for each day's victories. Keep a special praise section in your prayer journal. Just before retiring, evaluate your day and jot down praise points. Turn off the light, relax and drift off to sleep in an attitude of gratitude. From time to time, read through your praise journal. You'll see how faithful God is!

Family Plan: Instead of one person saying grace at mealtime, establish a family tradition of having each person interject a brief prayer of personal praise. Then dad or mom can finish the prayer with thanksgiving for the food. You'll help your children recognize God's blessings, and when guests are present, this will be a gentle way of saying "in this household, we love the Lord."

Let us run with perseverance the race marked out for us. Let us fix our eyes on Jesus, the author and perfector of our faith. (Hebrews 12:1-2)

FOURTH QUARTER FUMBLES
CHAPTER 9
MANASSEH:
The Come-back King

A team with heart

The 2007 baseball season was in its final weeks. On September 15, the Colorado Rockies were only four games above .500 and 6½ games behind in the race for a playoff spot. In other words, no one expected them to get there.

But, as you've probably heard, anything's possible in baseball.

To make it to the playoffs, the Rockies had to win 14 out of 15 final games. No one thought it would happen. But it did! October arrived, and this team was on a roll. And, to make a long story short, the Rockies went against the Red Sox in the World Series. If you're a baseball fan, you know the story ends here for the Rockies. Or does it?

Let me tell you something you probably don't know about the Colorado Rockies. This team is the first major league sports franchise organized and operated on the basis of Christian principles. And while that doesn't mean that the Rockies only sign Christian players, it does mean that they do the best they can to get players and employees with moral values. Then, they reinforce these values by doing things like placing scriptures in the weight room. And holding prayer and fellowship groups every Tuesday.

Summer of 2006 was a sad time for the Rockies. They lost a minor league coach when a line drive foul ball struck and killed him as he was coaching at first base. The Rockies players voted a full share of the team's 2007 playoff money for that coach's family, which includes two small sons who are learning from these baseball heroes. Now that's what I call a winning team! ("Winning the Right Way, The Colorado Rockies")

READ ALL ABOUT IT:

2 Chronicles 33.

O ne day recently I received a troubling wake-up call. Only it didn't come to me by way of the telephone. It came in a thick envelope that landed in my mailbox.

When I opened the envelope, there it was—tangible and troubling proof that, if I'm not already *in* the fourth quarter of my life, I'm certainly getting close. The unwelcome evidence was a membership card—from AARP. (Just in case you're too young to know about AARP, the acronym stands for American Association of Retired Persons).

As I examined the card, I felt stunned. At first I thought, "This must have been mailed to me by mistake, right? I mean, it seems like only yesterday that I was a teenager—hanging out with my buddies with no worries and no responsibilities." Then I remembered how many candles were on my last birthday cake (or *should* have been anyway), and my heart sank in resignation. The undeniable truth is that I've entered that age group that qualifies me to receive mail from AARP. I can't believe the years have gone by so fast, and I wish I could recapture some of them. But I can't. So I nursed my wounds and tried to draw comfort from that old advertising slogan. (You know, the one about getting better, not older.) It wasn't working, but I admit that I felt encouraged when I read the list of benefits on the AARP card—especially the one about *Confronting Age Discrimination by Employers*. (This could definitely come in handy next time the younger pastors on our church staff start messing with me!)

All kidding aside, time really is fleeting. The days can slip away from us "like sand in an hourglass." That's why it's imperative to make the most of the days God gives us—from start to finish. If King Manasseh were reading this book right now, I have a feeling he might say, "Amen!" This was a man who wasted a lot of the days God gave him before he learned this valuable lesson. Have you ever had one of those days that started off badly—and just got progressively worse? Manasseh's life was like one of those bad days. Unlike the other kings we've studied, he fumbled from the start. (Actually, it would be more accurate to say that he fouled.) He wasn't one of those people who just make a few poor impulsive choices as a teenager. He was downright bad and outright rebellious. Even worse, he influenced others to be that way, too.

That's just fair-warning for what you're about to read. You may even wonder why I bothered to put a chapter in this book about someone like Manasseh who seems so utterly evil and without a hint of a redeeming attribute. Hang in there with me! You may find Manasseh's story is the one you need to hear most.

A BAD, BAD BOY

Like I've already suggested, Manasseh was one bad boy. And this is most surprising, considering he was the son of Hezekiah—among the most godly and wonderful kings in the lineup. As you recall, God granted Hezekiah fifteen extra years of life. Some might say that one of the unfortunate events that happened during those years was the birth of Manasseh.

Bible scholars often call Hezekiah Judah's "second Solomon" because of his glorious reign and the good he accomplished for God. On the flip side, those same scholars sometimes refer to his son Manasseh as the "Ahab of Judah." Believe me, this is no compliment! Ahab was a notoriously wicked man whose kingship was marked by despicable acts. Along with his evil wife Jezebel, Ahab is remembered as the monarch who caused the northern kingdom of Israel to be dragged into exile by the Assyrians in 722 B.C. Let me tell you

136

some of the reasons why Manasseh has a similarly notorious reputation in the history of the southern kingdom of Judah.

THE DARK SIDE

Manasseh was twelve years old when Hezekiah died. I don't know if pre-adolescents in those days were as confused and vulnerable as they are these days, but it's safe to assume that Manasseh became king at a time when he was immature and impressionable. In 2 Chronicles 33:2 it says that Manasseh "did evil in the eyes of the Lord, following the detestable practices of the nations the Lord had driven out before the Israelites." Imagine being remembered for *undoing* God's work. Prior to Manasseh's rule, God brought the kingdom of Israel against the pagan Canaanites in order to judge them for being sold out to Satan—and to purge their culture from immersion in the occult.

Perhaps this would be a good time to insert a brief sidebar on an issue that many people have with God. It's important to deal with this issue head on because it's one that causes people to keep their distance from God. Despite our society's fascination with bloody action movies (box office numbers don't lie), we are confused and even filled with righteous indignation over the stories of violence and bloodshed we read in the Old Testament—particularly when scenes of carnage are painted under the banner of "God's will." We recoil at what we read and hurl accusations like, "If God is loving and good, how could He allow, much less approve of, this killing?" There is no easy answer to this question, and the bottom line ultimately is that God is sovereign—period. He does not owe us an explanation of why He allows or wills any event on earth. Faith is only faith, after all, when we choose to trust God merely because He *is* God—despite our human inability to understand His ways.

It does help broaden our spiritual vision, though, if we look carefully at these judgments that seem so harsh to us and examine them in the context of what was happening in the early days of *HIS*tory. After the fall of Adam and Eve, Satan came on in a mad rush to claim ownership of humanity. He had won a significant battle, but the war was just beginning. Who started the war? It wasn't God. This whole bloody mess (no pun intended) was man's choice, not God's. He could have washed His hands and let Satan take the spoils—the very soul of mankind. But that would be like a father giving up on a disobedient child who wandered into the street during rush hour. No dad would sit passively by and leave his child to get smashed to pieces by a speeding car. And God, who loves His children even more than we love ours, wouldn't do that either. He went to battle for us, and the war is still raging today. Sometimes the combat takes place in the unseen realm of Heaven. Other times, the fighting breaks out here on earth—violent, bloody fights that result in killing. The innocent get hurt. Even innocent children.

Putting this in the context of Manasseh's story, God had taken great pains to use Judah (and, at times, other nations) to legislate judgment on Satan and sin. Somehow, we are more comfortable with God's judgment when He legislates it directly (like fire raining down from Heaven or the great flood, for example). It's more obvious that way that the battle is "bigger" than we are. In this context, it's not about people fighting people. It's about right fighting wrong—like in a superhero movie. Still, like it or not, God sometimes uses human armies to enforce superhuman justice.

This is what had happened between Israel and the Canaanites prior to Manasseh's coming to the throne. Unfortunately, the adolescent king decided to challenge God's verdict. He did this by adopting the practices of the nations Israel had driven out. Undoing the widespread reforms instituted by his father, Manasseh:

- rebuilt the high places Hezekiah had torn down;

- erected altars to idols throughout Judah;

- worshiped astrology;

- built altars to false gods in the temple;

- carved an idol and placed it in God's house;

- practiced sorcery and witchcraft;

- consulted mediums and spiritists.

These are certainly offensive acts that dishonored, defied and angered God. Even more shocking to us is the record that confirms how "he sacrificed his sons in the fire in the Valley of Ben Hinnom" (2 Chronicles 33:6). As a father, this makes my blood run cold. I shudder at the thought of this scene. It is beyond my comprehension that a dad could actually issue an order to take a giant statue of a ghastly idol called Molech and heat it until it was red hot. Then, that he could take his own baby boy, so tiny and innocent, and place that helpless little one in the arms of that smoldering idol is simply unthinkable. Anyone who could stand and watch their child burn to death and listen to his tortured and terrified wails—well, I'm sure you agree that this is the ultimate evil. Yet, Manasseh practiced this horrific atrocity.

What could make a person do such a thing? I truly don't know. Yet, sometimes I turn on the news and hear about atrocious acts of child abuse, domestic violence and cruelty that are no less despicable. Like other people throughout the ages, Manasseh was so deluded by the dark side that he jumped right into that black hole. The many detestable acts attributed to him make grim reading. A sad summary of his life can be found in 2 Chronicles 33:6, which says: "He did much evil in the eyes of the Lord, provoking Him to anger."

AN EPIDEMIC OF SIN

Perhaps the most disturbing fact about Manasseh's life is the way he took others down with him. Have you ever known someone who tried to justify a wrong behavior by saying, "It's my life and my choice. I'm not hurting anybody else, so what's the big deal?" This might be a viable argument for someone marooned on a desert island where there is no one to get caught in the crossfire of poor choices and selfish acts. However, the truth is that no one lives in a vacuum. No matter how much we might like to think that our behavior won't impact other people, it's simply not true. As king, Manasseh's sinful deeds had tragic results for his own family, the entire nation of Judah and even nearby cultures. Like a contagious virus, one man's sin spread like wildfire and infected many, as we learn from 2 Chronicles 33:9, which says that, "Manasseh led Judah and the people of Jerusalem astray, so that they did **more** evil than the nations the Lord had destroyed before the Israelites."

The reign of Manasseh was like an epidemic of sin, sweeping through his world. Some years later, Jesus warned His disciples about the consequences of this type of scenario when He said, "Things that cause people to sin are bound to come, but woe to that person through whom they come. It would be better for him to be thrown into the sea with a millstone tied around his neck than for him to cause one of these little ones to sin" (Luke 17:12).

For 52 years, Manasseh caused his people to sin. In light of this, it's amazing that God gave him chance after chance to reverse the trend. 2 Chronicles 33:10 says, "The Lord spoke to Manasseh and his people, *but they paid no attention*." Despite his utter depravity, God loved Manasseh enough to send people to confront him and give him a chance to turn back. Sadly, the warnings fell on deaf ears and bloody retaliation was levied on the very messengers of mercy God sent to deliver these warnings. One of them, the great prophet Isaiah, was executed by Manasseh's decree. According to tradition, this mighty man of God, a friend of Manasseh's own father, was stretched out and cut in two with a saw. What a cruel and heartless man Manasseh was. His sin was incomprehensibly great. Amazingly, God's grace was greater.

ENOUGH IS ENOUGH

If God had zapped Manasseh with a lightning bolt, we'd cheer and applaud and feel like he got what he deserved. But God waited—and waited. If there ever was a story that points out our Heavenly Father's long-suffering mercy, this one does. Yet, the time came when even God's patience was tested to the breaking point. Hear what He had to say, as recorded in 2 Kings 21:10-15:

> The Lord said through his servants the prophets: "Manasseh king of Judah has committed these detestable sins. He has done more evil than the Amorites who preceded him and has led Judah into sin with his idols. Therefore this is what the Lord, the God of Israel, says: I am going to bring such disaster on Jerusalem and Judah that the ears of everyone who hears of it will tingle. I will stretch out over Jerusalem the measuring line used against Samaria and the plumb line used against the house of Ahab. I will wipe out Jerusalem as one wipes a dish, wiping it and turning it upside down. I will forsake the remnant of my inheritance and hand them over to their enemies. They will be looted and plundered by all their foes, because they have done evil in my eyes and have provoked me to anger from the day their forefathers came out of Egypt until this day."

I wonder what Manasseh felt when he heard these words. I don't know about you, but adrenalin would be pumping fear through every vein in my body and my shaky knees would be hard-pressed to hold me up. Not Manasseh! He and his nation were too sin-sick at this point to pay much attention. I think the horrors just went on for a while longer. In fact, 2 Kings 2:16 says that "Manasseh also shed so much innocent blood that he filled Jerusalem from end to end—besides the sin that he had caused Judah to commit, so that they did evil in the eyes of the Lord."

TURNING ON THE HEAT

There is a saying that people don't change when they see the light, but they do change when they feel the heat. As a pastor, I've seen the truth of this many times—in the lives of others and in my own life, too. I wish I was so completely responsive to the Spirit of God that when He enlightened me about something through scripture or other means, I'd receive it, believe it and change immediately. Occasionally that does happen. But I have to admit that more often, God has to turn on the heat to get me to take action. And I know from counseling others that I'm not unique. What amazes me is that, even though God knows this about us, He loves us so much that He patiently gives us the chance to see the light before He turns on the heat. When we don't respond that way, we force Him to apply *tough* love to bring us around. Sometimes, when we are too rushed to listen, He has to allow hard things to happen to get us focused on what's truly important. It's really our choice. You see, we have some control over how we relate to God. We can be engaged with Him, or detached. He wants to deal gently with us, but sometimes we force Him to apply some serious discipline. When the heat's on, it's—well, *HOT!* But God turns on the heat for our own good. That's exactly what He did with Manasseh.

NATIONAL DISASTER

As I suggested earlier in this chapter, Manasseh's story is like the flip side of the others we've been looking at. He had a horrific start. But now you'll see (and be utterly amazed) that Manasseh finished strong. Unfortunately, to bring this king across the finish line God had to turn the heat *way* up. Manasseh got burned pretty bad. Sadly, so did the entire nation of Judah. The refining fire God applied came in the form of a national disaster. Because of Manasseh's evil deeds, "the Lord brought against them the army commanders of the king of Assyria, who took Manasseh prisoner, put a hook in his nose, bound him with bronze shackles and took him to Babylon" (2 Chronicles 33:11).

This was the cleansing judgment that God had warned the people of Judah about. Yet still they did not pay attention. So at last, after years of long-suffering patience, God sent them away from Jerusalem and into bondage within a hostile culture. Finally, Manasseh got what he deserved. Or did he? Let's read on and see what it says in verses 11-12:

> In his distress [Manasseh] sought the favor of the Lord his God and humbled himself greatly before the God of his fathers. And when he prayed to him, the Lord was moved by his entreaty and listened to his plea; so he brought him back to Jerusalem and to his kingdom. Then Manasseh knew that the Lord is God.

In the opening sentence, I wish that word "distress" was "success." It isn't. God had to resort to very drastic measures before Manasseh was helpless. Only then did he finally realize how much he needed God and when he did, what happened? Manasseh cried out to God and was completely transformed. Gone was the arrogant, self-focused man. Now he was humble, prayerful and repentant. The change in Manasseh was radical, and it was authentic. We know this because of the way God responded mercifully to him and brought him back home to Jerusalem.

Right about now you may be saying, "Wait a minute! You're kidding me, right? This is just not fair. How could God forgive this jerk, Manasseh?" From a purely human perspective, you'd be absolutely right—but you see, God's ways are not human ways. This is one of those accounts like I mentioned earlier when we have a hard time reconciling God's actions with our own. In this story of Manasseh, we are forced to draw the conclusion that *anybody* is eligible for grace. What if you opened your morning paper tomorrow and saw these headlines: *Notorious ISIS leader embraces Christianity!* What if the article that followed mentioned that this murderous leader would be pardoned for all the deaths he was responsible for orchestrating? Or what if Adolph Hitler, guilty of having 6 million Jews executed during the Holocaust, cried out for mercy just before he died—like the thief on the cross next to Jesus. Remember what Jesus said to that thief? "Today you will see me in Paradise" (Luke 23:43).

This is a bitter pill to swallow, isn't it? We want God to show no mercy to people like Herod and Hitler. However, when he sees a repentant heart, His mercy flows. As I grapple with this, it helps me to think of God's pardon of Manasseh as a kind of redemption of the suffering that this evil man had caused others. You see, when God retrieves a horrible sinner like this, it's a huge blow to our enemy Satan. Most importantly, God's grace for an unworthy man like Manasseh means there is hope for all of us.

People often come to me with heavy hearts over things they've done in the past. They acknowledge that God has taken care of it on the Cross. They know intellectually that they are forgiven. But they don't feel it in their hearts. Do you feel that way today? Is there something from your past that makes you assume you are ineligible for God's amazing grace? Then let me ask you this question:

If God forgave Manasseh, don't you think He will forgive you?

The answer is "Yes!" Pause for a moment now and prayerfully let this wonderful and encouraging truth trickle down from your head to your heart. Close your eyes and think about the one thing in your life you feel most guilty about. That bad decision you made when you were a teenager. The person you hurt by your selfish actions. A deep, dark secret that haunts you like a ghost. Then think of Manasseh. The man who sacrificed his baby boy to an idol. The man who led a whole nation astray. If God can forgive an utter scoundrel like Manasseh, he can absolutely forgive you. He wants to and He will. Receive this good news like you would receive an unexpected and undeserved inheritance of money—with an elated heart. A heart set free. Then when Satan comes at you with those old ugly accusations (as he surely will), be prepared to laugh at him as you remind him about Manasseh and claim your own right to redemption in Christ. You see, redemption is not only something Jesus did *for us once* on the Cross. It's something He does *daily through us* as we let go of our guilt and allow His grace and love to shine through us and draw others to Him.

A HAPPY ENDING WITH UNHAPPY CONSEQUENCES

I love happy endings to sad stories, don't you? We have one here, don't we? However, let me make one thing perfectly clear. Just because God forgave Manasseh does not mean everyone lived happily ever after. God forgives sin, but He doesn't capriciously cancel the consequences. Even though Manasseh's conversion motivated him to spend the remainder of his life doing good, there was still a very negative legacy that impacted Judah for years to come. In 2 Chronicles 33:14-20 we see how Manasseh attempted to undo this legacy by getting rid of idolatry, restoring God's altar, and telling Judah to serve the Lord. Tragically, it was too late for many of the people he influenced. They had developed sinful habits that they never gave up. Manasseh's earlier evil influence was like a stubborn infection that just wouldn't go away. In fact, the prophets refer more often to the sin of Manasseh than any of the other kings. This is how he's immortalized in biblical history; this is the logical consequence to the way he lived most of his life.

Let's put this in perspective within the goal of this book. What key to finishing well do we learn from Manasseh? First of all, it's always best to play well from start to finish. As we just said, there are inescapable consequences for playing a sloppy game. Please don't look at Manasseh and say to yourself, "This is great! I can live any way I want to and come back from behind at the end of my life." This is not the way a believer should live.

On the other hand, if you are already nearing the end of your game and you haven't played it well, take heart from Manasseh. He came to God late, but still he came. He found forgiveness. He found peace. He found hope. God, in His mercy, was even gracious enough to pull back some of the pieces and put them together to fulfill some of His original purpose for Manasseh. That's the kind of God we serve. He doesn't toss the baby out with the bath water! What He did for Manasseh, he can do for you and for me. As the encouraging lyrics of a wonderful hymn reminds us:

> *Grace, grace, God's grace,*
> *Grace that will pardon and cleanse within;*
> *Grace, grace, God's grace,*
> *GRACE THAT IS GREATER THAN*
> *ALL OUR SIN.*
> *(Lyrics, Daniel A. Towner)*

PLAYING BY THE BOOK
Guilt Busters

God has placed Manasseh's story in the Bible to show that no matter how low we go, He is there to lift us up when we sincerely turn to Him for forgiveness. One of the greatest encouragements about this story is the way God redeemed Manasseh's terrible past—and gave him a second chance.

Worship Workout

D o you need a second chance? Does guilt and the remembrance of past sins keep you from enjoying the freedom Jesus purchased for you on the cross? If so, use the prayer below as a guide to help you seek the sweet release of His inner peace. This is His gift to you, but you must believe it and receive it.

Prayer for Inner Peace

Father, I am tormented by guilt. I can't shake the memory of these sins without Your help:

_____

_____

_____

_____

Today I bring these sins to you with an earnest desire to be released from crippling guilt. I am emboldened by the story of Manasseh to think that if You forgave him, then maybe you will forgive me. I thank You that I am invited into Your presence because of what Jesus did on the Cross. I humbly claim Him as my Savior for the complete forgiveness of my sins—buried in the sea, placed behind Your back. And now, Lord, I ask You to set me free from this distracting and destructive guilt. Replace it with Your peace and free me to fulfill Your purpose in my life. Redeem the time I've wasted and, from this day forward, help me to be a contagious Christian who draws others to You. I pray this in Jesus' name. Amen.

If we confess our sins, he is faithful and just and will forgive us our sins and purify us from all unrighteousness. (1 John 1:9)

FOURTH QUARTER FUMBLES

CHAPTER 10

How to be an MVP

You are invited to join . . .

GOD'S HALL OF FAME

You are cordially invited to a banquet to celebrate your life as a good and faithful servant of God.

Date: The day you leave this earth

Time: The moment you arrive in Heaven

Place: Kingdom of Heaven Banquet Hall

At the entrance, an angel will be waiting to escort you to a special table for honored guests.

Reservation required—No exceptions!

Please contact Jesus Christ to make yours.

"Well done, good and faithful servant!"
—Matthew 25:21a

READ ALL ABOUT IT:

A s I write this final chapter, it's late summer. Another football season is about to kick off. For some players, it will be their starting season—the fulfillment of a dream. For others, this will be the season when they achieve their personal best. It will be just the opposite for the ones who fumble and get taken out of the game. There will be a few who will play that inevitable last game this season.

The truth is, an athlete's career is pretty short. Sure, some are remembered, long into the future. A few—the best of the best—are inducted into the Hall of Fame. But far more play hard, finish their careers at a relatively young age, retire, and move on to do something else. As new players take the field, most retirees will be forgotten.

In this respect, life is a lot like football. When we are young, the years seem to stretch out before us. We mistakenly think we've got all the time in the world. From the moment we're born, the clock is ticking. Our time on earth *will* run out. The fourth quarter will sneak up and everyone's destiny ends with a ten-second countdown. When those last seconds of life come, will you be ready?

I have good news for you. God doesn't want you to live, die, and be forgotten. Did you read the invitation at the beginning of this chapter? It may seem a little flippant, or even trite. However, I hope it makes you stop and think—because, you really are invited to join God's Hall of Fame. If you choose to accept, He truly does have a celebration planned in your honor. Jesus, as King of Kings, invites every person to come to His Heavenly Hall of Fame and live with

Him there forever. If you haven't already talked to him about your reservation, don't wait a minute longer! Here's what you need to do.

GOD IS WAITING FOR YOUR CALL

Did you know that God loves you so much that He personally came to earth and made a way of salvation from death *for you?* Here's the best news you'll ever read:

> For God so loved the world that he gave his one and only Son, that whoever believes in him shall not perish but have eternal life. For God did not send his Son into the world to condemn the world, but to save the world through him. (John 3:16)

Once you believe this truth, there are three simple steps God asks you to take:

First, you must admit your condition to Him. Romans 3:23 says, "For all have sinned and fall short of the glory of God." No one is sinless except God Himself. All He asks is that you admit it. As a parent, wouldn't you want your child to come to you and confess a wrongdoing? Only then could you forgive and help correct their misbehavior. If you have never admitted your condition to your Heavenly Father, will you do so now?

Then, you must recognize Jesus Christ as God's only solution to your condition. Jesus said, "I am *THE* way, *THE* truth and *THE* life. No one comes to the Father except through me" (John 14:6). In our culture, where freedom of choice is a cherished human right, some people struggle with this. They want to believe that any path they choose leads to God's house but that's simply not what He says.

I am not going to spend time here defending God's position. After all, He is absolutely sovereign and has the right to make His own "house" rules. God never owes us an explanation—but, if you are interested, He will show you His reasons and the wisdom behind them as you study scripture with a teachable heart. Do you believe Jesus Christ is the way to be right with God? If so, then take the final step.

Receive Jesus as your Savior and Lord. You may be wondering how to do this. The Bible says, "to all who believe in His name, He gave the right to become children of God" (John 1:12). All you have to do is ask! You can do that right now by praying a simple prayer like this:

> *Dear God, thank You for sending Your son, Jesus Christ, to earth. I believe Jesus was who He said He was and proved it by rising from death. I want to discover and begin following Your plan and purpose for my life. I want to get to know You personally. Thank You, Jesus Christ, for dying for me and forgiving all my sins. I receive You as my Lord and Savior. Thank You for your free gift of eternal life.*

Three simple steps. That's all it takes to secure your reservation to Heaven. If you have now received Christ as your Savior and Lord, I urge you to tell someone right away. This is the beginning of your *eternal* lifetime! By letting someone know, you will be more likely to move forward with God and not look back. You might even help someone else take these life-changing steps.

SAINTS vs SINNERS

Whether you're a rookie or a veteran Christian, the whole purpose of this book has been to help you discover the keys to playing by God's rules and finishing well. I hope you have found it helpful to look at the lives of Israel's godly kings who fumbled and fell. If you take to heart what you learned from their stories, you'll have a better chance at avoiding the mistakes they made. Still, let's be realistic. I'm sure you've heard that old saying. The one that goes: "Christians aren't perfect. They're just forgiven."

In my effort to equip you with the keys to finishing strong, I don't want to leave you with the impression that you have to play a perfect game in order to be received into Heaven. That's impossible in our fallen world. The criteria for making it into God's Hall of Fame is not based on living a perfect life. It's based on living a life of faith in Jesus Christ.

When you are ushered to the table of honor reserved for you at that heavenly celebration, you might be surprised who will be there. Along with Abraham and Isaac, Moses and Aaron, David and Solomon, Peter, John and Mary and all the other saints of the Bible, you'll meet average people who spent their days on earth doing ordinary things. But as they lived their ordinary lives, the extraordinary goal they looked towards was God.

Let me tell you about one of those ordinary people who lived an extraordinary life—a "saint" named William Bawden. Affectionately known as Uncle Bill to children and adults alike, Bill was a member of our church for many years. Sunday after Sunday you'd find him posted at the entrance to our sanctuary, dressed in a bright red sports coat and wearing a friendly smile. "Hello, young lady or young man!" he would say as he warmly shook the hands of boys and girls, men and women. His genuine delight made everyone feel like they were coming home. In fact, if Bill wasn't at his station on any given Sunday, people were concerned. Our famous greeter, Bill Bawden, was a living example that you don't have to be a pastor or a music director in order to have a ministry.

When Bill passed away at the age of 86, a local paper featured an article about him with some very interesting facts about his life.

Born on May 31, 1920 in Lena, Illinois, Bill came to California with his family when he was just a little boy. I'm not certain what happened, but Bill spent most of his childhood in an orphanage. Whatever those circumstances were, they did not hinder him from becoming a caring man and a good citizen. Bill served his country in the Navy and was a proud World War II veteran. After the war, he returned to California and earned a bachelor's degree in education at California State University in Los Angeles. His education continued at California Baptist Seminary, where he received a master of divinity degree.

Bill Bawden had a heart for children and felt called to be an educator. For 30 years, he taught school and his students loved him. A close friend said that when he walked into a classroom, "he became a human climbing tree." One student wrote, "Bill walks like an angel. He speaks like an eagle. His hair is white as snow . . . I love Bill because he loves me!"

When Bill retired, he continued to be a servant of others by volunteering hundreds of hours to a community service group. He helped provide Thanksgiving and Christmas dinners and birthday gifts and lunch outings for elementary school children. In 1992, the Claremont Unified School District honored him with the Intergenerational National Volunteer Award, which is reserved for individuals who work with students, teachers and administrators. ("William Bawden School Teacher, Community Volunteer")

By human standards, Bill did not achieve fame or fortune. He simply lived one day at a time with a single purpose — to glorify God and show His love to others by faithfully representing Him in all areas of his life. This is why I have no doubt that Bill was welcomed into Heaven with those coveted words from the Master:

Well done, good and faithful servant! You have been faithful with a few things; I will put you in charge of many things. Come and share your master's happiness! (Matthew 25:21)

FINISHING WELL

Now, at last, we've come to the punch line for this book. Here it is, the one thing I hope you'll remember: The key to finishing well is living well—and the key to living well is walking with Jesus. Moment by moment, day by day, year by year—a walk so close and intimate that His thoughts become your thoughts.

A few years ago, the mother of a friend of mine recently departed from this earth. As my friend likes to say, "She moved to Heaven." At 84, this woman was ready. For some years, her health had been failing. During the last few, she was housebound. There were good days and bad days, but not one of those days was spent in self-pity. When she wasn't asleep, this little dwindling saint spent most of her time sitting in a chair, reading her Bible and praying for her family.

One afternoon, my friend's mother slipped into a coma. The end was coming, and her children gathered around her bed, holding each other and praying. They thanked God for her love, her life of service, and the rich heritage of faith she was leaving for them. A short time later, almost like she had been waiting around to hear that prayer, she stopped breathing and passed on. Just before that final breath, my friend saw a faint smile on her mother's face and a slight nod of her head. It was as if someone only she could see had walked into the room and said, "Ready to go now?" And she said, "Yes."

A few days later, this memory came back to my friend during her early morning quiet time with God. Her mother's well-used Bible lay open in her lap. She turned the pages slowly, cherishing the notes her mom had written on page after page through many years of study. On the very last page, these words in shaky handwriting jumped out at her:

*As I grow older and spend most of my time talking
to God (rather than on the telephone) I hope I am
growing so close to Jesus that when I meet Him face
to face we will say, "As we were saying"—and continue our conversation.*

This is the way God wants every life to finish. With our loved
ones gathered around to send us off with a bittersweet blessing—and
Jesus to take our hand and walk us through the doorway to Heaven.
From this day on, may this be the goal you run towards, without a
single fumble.

CITATIONS

Chapter 1

"New York Giants: Miracle in the Meadowlands," September 15, 2007, http://en.allexperts.com/q/New-York-Giants-287/miracle-meadowlands.htm

Chapter 2

"Bill Buckner," Wikipedia-the free encyclopedia, September 15, 2007, http://en.wikipedia.org/wiki/Bill_Buckner

Chapter 3

"Romo's botched hold grounds Cowboys, lifts Seahawks," September 15, 2007, http://sports.espn.go.com/nfl/recap?gameID=270106026

Chapter 4

"Webber's timeout hands title to Carolina," September 15, 2007, http://sports.go.com/espn/espn25/story?page=moments/59

Chapter 5

"Jacobellis loses shot at gold with stumble," September 15, 2007, http://222.msnbc.msn.com/id/11403461/

Chapter 6

Hofstetter, Steve; "Just A Game? The tragic story of Donnie Moore," April 28, 2002, http://222.stevehofstetter.com/unpublished.cfm?ID=52

The Merriam-Webster Dictionary for Large Print Users, G.K. Hall & Co., Boston, MA, 1977, p. 784

God's Little Devotional Book for Women, prepared by W.B. Freeman Concepts; Tulsa, OK, ©1996, Honor Books, Inc., p. 16

Chapter 7

CEF (Child Evangelism Fellowship) Singapore, Wikipedia-the free encyclopedia

Chapter 8

"Bob Wieland," Wikipedia-the free encyclopedia, en.wikepedia. org/wiki/Bob_Wieland

Chapter 9

"Winning the Right Way, The Colorado Rockies," October 24, 2007, https://webmail.roadrunner.com/webedge/do/mail/message/view?msgld=INBOXDELIM . . .

Chapter 10

"William Bawden, School Teacher, Community Volunteer," Claremont Courier, January 31, 2007, p. 13

Good Medicine for Strategic Living

W hat do you do when your body warns you with a troubling symptom that something is wrong? You visit your physician and get a prescription for the right medicine, therapy or procedure to fix the problem before it becomes lethal.

The same principle applies to spiritual health. In the Bible, God prescribes antidotes to help prevent and overcome the spiritual "toxins" that, if left unchecked, can cripple and destroy us from the inside out.

Glenn Gunderson's first book, *Biblical Antidotes to Life's Toxins*, is good medicine for strategic living. Filled with sound biblical advice, practical suggestions, and relevant illustrations, this book can help face life's challenges head-on and avoid those fatal fumbles at any stage of your life.

CONNECT WITH US!

PURPOSE CHURCH
586 N. Main Street, Pomona, California 91768
909-629-5277
Lead Pastor – Glenn Gunderson

PURPOSE CHURCH CLAREMONT
Campus Pastor – Brian Holland

FIRST BAPTIST CHURCH OF KALISPELL, MONTANA
Pastor – Mary Todd

BAPTIST COMMUNITY CHURCH
of Arco, Idaho

MERCY ROAD CHURCH
Indianapolis, Indiana
mercyroad.cc
Lead Pastor – Josh Husmann

PurposeChurch.com
 Purpose Church   @purposepomona